Living with Depression & get you out of the fog,

A Self-Help book

(An Amanda Green Self-Help series: Book 1)

By Amanda Green

This book copyright ©Amanda Green

First edition published February 2016 by Amanda Green

ISBN-13: 978-1530105854

Cover art and design by Aidana WillowRaven

Copyright of the text produced herein remains the property of the writer and permission to publish is gratefully acknowledged by the author

All rights reserved

This book is based on the author's experiences. The identities of others' within this book have been changed, although the information and events are true.

No parts of this publication may be reproduced, stored in a retrieval system, or transmitted in any form, by any means, electronic, mechanical, photocopying, recording or otherwise without prior permission of the copyright owner.

For Michael and my mum and dad

Strength and Love still get us through

xxxxxxx

5* review "Brilliant advice in this easy to read handy guide. It should be on everyone's shelf"

A bit about me…

I am Amanda Green, self-published author of seven inspiring books. Amanda Green is my pseudonym – my real name is Sandra Dean.

'My Alien Self: My Journey Back to Me' is my self-published memoir of my journey through mental illness to recovery. '39' is the sequel. I want to inspire others that it is possible to recover and have a life worth living. Many people do not understand mental illness and judge people unfairly, so I created www.amandagreenauthor.co.uk where I publish articles on the topics covered in my story and campaign to 'stop the stigma surrounding mental illness'. I also write thought provoking, inspiring fiction with the theme of overcoming adversities (abuse, homelessness, mental health, relationships and more)

I run three personal websites/blogs for which I write all copy and articles and provide all photography.

I have had my writing and photography work published in various magazines and local newspapers. I enjoy the challenge of getting published.

Aside from writing and social networking, I spend a lot of time with my pets; a handsome cat called Titus, a pretty kitten called Millie and two tanks of tropical fish. I strongly believe in pet animal therapy as being good for our mind, body and soul and I promote the fostering and adopting of animals as opposed to private breeding and purchase. I detest animal cruelty.

I love eating out and reviewing restaurants, travel, days out, campaigning for the precious Orang-utan and the issues of unsustainable palm oil production and seeing my family. I also enjoy reading, theatre, films, TV and cooking.

I have travelled on/off across the world, taking in twenty-five Countries - living and working at times in Japan, Thailand and Australia and have enjoyed a very mixed bag of jobs.

I am just finishing my level 4 Counselling skills Diploma at college and am BACP registered, as I would love to be able to help others' facing issues. My placement is with homeless people who need help to move on from their adversities, and I absolutely love it!

I regularly post blogs about coping strategies, inspirational things to do, Borderline Personality disorder, depression, Obsessive compulsive disorder, schizophrenia, paranoia, dissociation, psychosis, anxiety/panic attacks, thyroid issues, eating disorders (Anorexia Nervosa and Bulimia), alcohol and drug abuse, sexual abuse/rape, Quetiapine (Seroquel anti-psychotics) and Citalopram (anti-depressant) and therapies such as Cognitive behavioural therapy (CBT) - all of which I have experienced in one way or another either myself, or those I know have. Also information on mental health charities, forums, campaigns, the stigma surrounding mental illness, some of my personal experiences, celebrities with mental health issues and mental health in the family.

For this book, I am concentrating on Depression and Anxiety, which often co-occur, and in sharing information, personal experiences and many ways to cope with both, I hope I will be able to help you to live better too!

First of all, let's talk depression… Depression is something I still live with. I have managed to find a whole range of coping mechanisms that work for me, reducing any bouts to a day or two at most. Below is some information about Depression.

Depression symptoms, information and help to get better

There are many forms of depression, which can have a negative effect on; moods and emotions, thinking patterns and how a person views life as a whole, physical fitness and energy levels, the ability to concentrate and/or sleep and interest in sex. At the lower end of the scale, it could describe a period of being in low spirits, which could impact on the quality of things that people do, but wouldn't affect the day to day activities that they carry out. At the other end of the scale, depression can affect a sufferer in a much more adverse way – stopping the normal functioning in life and sometimes the loss of life if the person gives up on their struggle completely.

Symptoms of depression

Psychological symptoms:

• Depressed mood, which incorporates feeling low, sad, guilty or numb

• Increased anxiety and worry about things that may not have caused anxiety in the past

• A low self esteem

• Crying and sadness

• Persistent negative thoughts. This can be distracting and the lack of concentration it causes can affect a person's memory, which in turn can lead to frustration.

• Increased anger and feeling irritable, perhaps with an increased intolerance of others

• Confusion and inability to decide and be clear about goals

• Decreased enjoyment of activities or lack of interest in activities that were once enjoyed

• A reduced sex drive

• The inability to enjoy or take part in activities and confusion about life can lead to self-criticism where a person can believe that they are worthless, inadequate, bad, useless, and disliked

• A sense of hopelessness can prevail in severe cases where there is a strong belief that there is no hope of being happy again and no point in carrying on. The person can lose any desire to help themselves and this can lead to consideration of suicide or even suicide itself.

• Psychosis (loss of reality, delusions, hallucinations, feeling of running on automatic) can occur if the stress and anxiety gets too much.

Physical symptoms:

• A loss of energy is common, with the person feeling tired very often

• Eating patterns can be affected, with the person either eating much more or less than usual

• IBS and constipation can occur, as the stress levels affect the gut and bowel.

- General fitness is reduced, and aches and pains are very common

- The menstrual cycle can be affected

- Lack of sleep – either difficulty getting to sleep or waking up very early – this will also affect the person's energy levels and can turn into insomnia

- Loss of interest in sex

Social symptoms:

- All these negative symptoms can affect a person's abilities and concentration at work

- Withdrawing from social activities and friends, due to irritability, lack of motivation and inability to concentrate.

- Not taking part in previous past times

- Difficulties in relationships with family, friends and work colleagues

What can affect the chances of getting depression?

• Possibly an underactive thyroid – a person with an underactive thyroid has a slower metabolic rates than others, which can cause lethargy, weight gain and depression

• Some recreational drugs can influence the chances of depression

• Physical illness, low fitness levels and poor diet can all promote depression

• Losing a parent when young

• A person who has very low self esteem

• A single mother who does not have much support

• A person with a repetitive cycle of negative life experiences (divorce, moving house or job, loss of earnings etc)

• Long periods of unemployment

• Those who live in cities

• Abusive or neglectful childhoods

• A person who do not have a supportive network

• Unresolved mourning of the death or loss of someone close

• Major life changes such as changing jobs, divorce etc

• Loss of job or status

The list is endless really, and sometimes a depressive episode is short lived, other times the depression stays with someone all their lives.

Depression can form a vicious circle, whereby a person can feel even more depressed about having depression in the first place. Negative thoughts about the inner depression and the outside world can get out of control, and the depressive symptoms can get more severe as time goes on if the cycle is not stopped. The initial cause of the depression can get lost in the process, as the depression wreaks havoc on one's life.

Thought processes that can occur

Black and white thinking – everything is black or white, with no grey areas; good or bad with no in between or mix. If a person fails an exam, they may think they are useless, which is not true; they just failed one exam. Someone does something the person doesn't like and they think 'He's a horrible person' when there is no proof of this.

Generalising – when something is wrong, a person might think that EVERYTHING is wrong, when it is not the truth. A negative thought is carried over into many other areas and positive things can be thought of as negatives. Looking on the dark side of everything and jumping to conclusions.

Living by rules – Making unrealistic rules and expectations about life and how a person 'should' be can lead to disappointment, guilt and a feeling of failure. 'Should've' and 'could've' are negative expectations about the past, whereas 'can' and 'will' are positive thoughts about the future.

Catastrophising – When an event occurs, the person might see if for far more than it is; how bad or how awful. In this case, the prediction of failure or real disaster are over estimated.

Some other types of depression are:

Bipolar Disorder (previously named manic depression) -- This disorder is defined by a cyclical change of mood from mania (severe highs and excitability) and depression (low mood).

Psychotic depression -- When depression is very severe, it can lead to delusions and possibly hallucinations (psychosis). Psychosis can also occur when someone has tried to dissociate from an upsetting event. Trying to forget about an event, but not dealing with it can cause psychosis to occur.

Post-natal depression -- depression which occurs between 2 weeks and up to a year after giving birth,

SAD (seasonal affective disorder) -- Usually linked to the winter, this depression occurs with lack of sunlight. The person will wish to sleep more and eat more carbohydrates.

Treatments for depression

Getting over depression can take some time and needs commitment, strength and energy to overcome the symptoms. Working on negative thoughts is very important, as depression is like a computer virus in a way – it feeds itself and multiplies. By that, I mean that a negative thought can lead to a negative action and behaviour. The outcome from the negative behaviour and action can lead to more negative thoughts about oneself or the world around us. This can soon go on and on and spiral into a deep depression. The worse one gets, the deeper into depression they get. It is hard, at times, to find the positive thoughts and actions in oneself, but you have to really want to change your life and feel better and imagine a happier life to keep you going.

Things that can get in the way of recovery:

BEING IN DENIAL – This occurs when a person just cannot or will not accept that they have depression or anxiety, and therefore, cannot or will not seek help. Even if a person does seek help, how much they are 'helped' will depend upon how much the person believes that they need to change and are willing to make the effort to change. If a person believes that events and the subsequent depression are everyone else's fault except theirs, they are in denial. The person will need to accept their depression and accept events that are out of their control. With acceptance, comes the desire to do more positive things, such as seeking the right kind of help, admitting to oneself and others' that 'I have some issues' and then facing the depression head on in order to fight it. I believe mental disorder is part of the 'make-up' of a person, therefore the goal is not to 'get rid of all symptoms' and set out an unachievable task, but to work with each symptom by way of priority, in order to be able to cope with, or even eradicate the symptom itself. Living in a world of stating that everything bad that happens to a person is because of other people, is never going to work. NO ONE CAN BE HELPED IF THEY ARE IN DENIAL. Once a person comes out of denial, they can seek help, start to understand how to help themselves, share their burden and find a way to have a 'life worth living'.

'YOU LOOK ALRIGHT' - A major issue which can hinder the process of getting help, particularly from the NHS, a workplace or within a close circle of friends and family, is when, to the outside world, the person *looks alright*. But the thing is, a person can be a master at covering up their real emotions, and the outside world do not see them when they are indoors, suffering at times. If a person dresses nicely and do their hair, or smile a lot, it can seem like life is treating the person well. The human race can be masters at smiling through adversity, and using different personas for different people or experiences, so it is not surprising that the audience do not recognise or accept the underlying, negative issues being covered up. This persona issue can very much stop a person from getting help or support of any kind. If the act is dropped, and a person can be more honest and real about their feelings, it will be much easier to gain understanding and support from those who matter.

To get help the person needs to come to terms with their problem, take it on as their own, and seek help.

Don't be scared to tell people as there's nothing to be ashamed of!

So, let's get started with helping you!

I have laid this book out from A to Z, which makes it easier to navigate through and locate sections you may wish to re-read. It is all about helping yourself. I want to show you, through each chapter, all the techniques I have discovered (through experience) that have helped me to cope with or recover from depression and anxiety symptoms. Now that I have a life worth living again, I want to share with you how I did it, so that you can too!

A is for…

A word about stigma

I firstly want to talk about stigma. Stigma can come in the guise of bullying, but can also just be an individual not understanding someone else's mental illness and avoiding them or invalidating them. It comes in so many more forms than that, and is usually borne from lack of understanding, lack of knowledge or ignorance, but whatever way it is delivered, it is nearly always destructive.

> Think before you act, and learn before you judge

No-one wants to be mentally ill any more than a person wants to have a physical illness. People empathise with illnesses or adversities they can understand or see, physically, such as cancer, Parkinson's or an amputated limb, because they can imagine what it is like. A person without a mental illness may only begin to understand those who do, by finding out what it feels like, how the mind can work for those people, and why they might do the things they do.

For example, many people under-estimate the force of depression – "Oh yeah, she just needs to deal with it" they may think or say. I was told this by some friends and family, and it made me feel even more alone. Education is needed to help more people understand what it really feels like to suffer with depression, and other mental health disorders, as many think individuals are making it up, because they cannot 'see' it.

Stigma against people with mental illness hurts them. It can make them worse. It can even make people take their own lives. Mentally ill people should not feel ashamed of themselves or their illness any more than anyone else with a physical illness.

The kindest thing anyone can do for a person with mental illness is to be 'anti-stigma', by trying to understand the person's illness and creating empathy for that person. It's not about sympathy; it's about empathy – really trying to understand things from the other person's point of view.

Social networking and personal blogs are a valid addition to the world of mental illness and mental health. Not only do professionals share their knowledge but sufferers and families of sufferers are sharing the stories of their journeys through mental illness more and more. This not only brings the subject out in the open, it helps people to understand mental illness. Mental health issues are often misunderstood because they cannot be seen physically, unlike physical issues (broken leg, cut or burn) or physical illnesses, such as Influenza, cancer or Parkinson's disease.

Although there are symptom lists for each mental illness, people are individual and when it comes to the brain, it can depend upon the person's base personality make-up to start with as to how a mental illness will affect them. Of course this is not always the case, but quite prevalent with personality disorders, as I know myself.

However, symptoms are not the subject of this chapter – stories and stigma are.

The subject of stigma is one which, thankfully, many people are now fighting. Mental health charities, advocates and many individuals are campaigning to stop others' negative attitudes to mental illness. They do this knowingly. However, unknowingly, some individuals are helping to cut stigma by way of writing on their personal blogs or social networking. Just by sharing our stories of mental illness, we are helping tackle the stigma that surrounds the subject.

I am very passionate about the campaign to fight stigma and so I wrote my memoir showing how my mental illness progressed from childhood, what it felt like to be ill, and my journey to getting better, but I also focussed on explaining stigma as well. I also share articles and personal experiences on my website/blog, on social networks Face book and Twitter and by sending stories to magazines, mental health charities and organisations.

Some of these sites have huge audiences and are very powerful in their messages about mental health.

So, I encourage all who read this, to get sharing – knowledge is power and sharing really does help to reduce stigma – do something today!

I have suffered stigma through my mum's schizophrenia from my childhood, and also my own illnesses. On top of a sometimes terrifying illness, a person needs support not to be called names or labelled. Stigma is NOT sociable and especially shows up on social networks; it makes the person look bad and is very unhelpful.

I have been the victim (I don't like to use that word but it is the best way to describe it) in many ways – from family, friends, my GP, psychiatrists, NHS and others. When I wanted help I got blanked, when I pretended I was fine I was incorporated. It doesn't make sense. My psychiatrist told my ex-boyfriend that I would be 'very difficult to live with' and that he shouldn't molly coddle my moods. All because I had Borderline Personality Disorder (BPD), one of the most stigmatised and least known about mental disorders. But 10% of sufferers commit suicide so those psychiatrists who believe it doesn't exist on the other hand are also wrong. They have little idea that is all. As a writer, I embarked on a few college courses and writing retreats but when looking to apply for a particular course in Spain I realised I couldn't apply, because I was on anti-depressant medications and had mental illnesses. I could understand why they wouldn't want to risk issues occurring for other guests but they 'painted us all with the same brush' as it were.

The fact is that one in four of us will experience some form of mental health issue, but in reality, I think, with today's fast paced and stressful environment and economy, there are far more than that, and many people live with mental health issues in ignorance, because the issues do not affect them enough to cause major problems with their life.

I experienced all sides of the spectrum of people's reactions when I first decided to talk about my mental health problems after years of silence. I admit I was not impressed by some of the reactions and they were most unhelpful to me.

Having depression or mental illness doesn't mean that one is mad or antisocial – on the contrary, many sufferers are kind hearted and docile. The media doesn't help either. For example, they have been known to suggest a person with schizophrenia is violent and a menace to society, which is misleading. In fact, sufferers are more likely to harm themselves than others and are not violent at all. Mental health illnesses portrayed in film and news are most often sensationalised, and this really should be stopped, as it is so unhelpful to sufferers and those around them who are getting the wrong idea.

When people talk about 'stigma of mental health' there really is one. The more I tried to 'come out' and talk to people about my problems, the more alienated I seemed to get. People preferred to glaze over it, telling me to get a grip, a job, or that I shouldn't hide behind illness. Charming! Since this was a very difficult obstacle to overcome, as I wanted to share my experiences, but was unable to find the right platform for it, I felt even more alone with my problems. No one seemed to understand or even want to. It was almost like I was making it all up.

When I went to seek help professionally, the obstacle became the way I looked – because I 'look alright' I can't be too bad. Yes, I do look alright, and if I was not I would stay indoors, but this is no reason to ignore someone's pleas for help.

People 'discriminate' against others with mental health problems and therefore are in effect confirming that the 'stigma' is true and correct, yet it clearly is not.

Something really needs to be done to ensure that this attitude changes for the benefit of all.

I would like to suggest that we take another stance on our thoughts on mental health, and realise that those who suffer from one also need care and charity from others, and some understanding for who they are. They are just like anyone else, apart from some of the things they think or feel; but they are not bad people or mad people.

Also, those with a problem need to speak out and tell others so that they can be supported, and not hide away and worry about what others will think or how they will react – there is a lot of support out there too!

I have learnt a lot about mental health issues from research and others. Sadness, guilt, happiness and a whole range of emotions are involved for those concerned.

One thing is very apparent: mental disorders are often not dealt with well by those who have not experienced them or know very little about them. It is like many things really – if we do not know about something, we either find out more about it or just ignore it, or even worse, we are scared of it and therefore rebel against it.

There are many other serious health problems, such as cancer, leukaemia or diabetes which, instead of scorn, lead to reactions from others such as care and charity, but mental health issues are no different – they are a problem for the person who has them, and it does not mean the person is 'mental', 'crazy', or a 'loony' and any other derogatory terms.

Some mental health problems are:

- Depression

- Bipolar disorder

- Schizophrenia

- Personality disorders

- Anxiety disorders

- Eating disorders

These problems are widespread (one in four people will experience mental health problems at some point in their lives), and many celebrities are now coming out as having things like depression, such as Ruby Wax, Alastair Campbell and Stephen Fry, so that it can be seen more clearly the amount of people who suffer and how to help them to get on.

Did you know that Winston Churchill, Abraham Lincoln, Florence Nightingale, Charles Darwin, and Marie Curie all had mental health problems? They did, yet they are well respected for their fantastic efforts in history for the good of men and women. Would this have changed if their problems were common knowledge? These days the answer is probably yes! But in a recent survey, only four out of ten employers said they would employ someone with a history of mental illness. People with depression are seen by some as 'being weak willed' or 'lazy and wanting time off work' or that they should be happy. Depression is not something that can be turned on or off, and those that really do suffer with it will tell you that they feel trapped inside themselves and wish they could turn it off.

Take responsibility for yourself; it's very rewarding.

B is for…

Being yourself – learn to know and love yourself and others

Have you ever wondered 'Who am I?' I have. So, I would like to look at some ways we might look at ourselves, using my own experiences.

Inferiority issues

It is very easy to feel inferior to others when we feel down or anxious and cannot do what we perceive others' can do easily. If we feel very down and at times useless, we can make up stories that people are thinking negatively about us. We hear what we want to hear and don't always hear what the person is really saying because something hits a chord with us and we concentrate on it so much we believe they are aiming their comments at us. We take what someone says personally, even if it wasn't aimed at us at all. At times, I have misconstrued what people have said to me. For example, someone could be talking about how easy they find it to cook, yet other people don't cook much anymore. Now, if I do not cook much because I just don't feel like it and I feel bad that I don't cook and am not healthy and it's on my mind… well, I could take what they have said as a personal insult. Because I have already berated myself for it, I might perceive that they are picking on me too. What I would need to do is to ask myself what the person really meant. Did they make the comment really about me, or were they generalising? Was it just that they struck a chord with my feeling of weakness without knowing it? In my experience, more often than not, I have misinterpreted others' comments to be a dig at me just because I was feeling low myself. So, ask yourself, am I making up a story here, before jumping to conclusions.

And just because other people can do things or have experienced things/know things we do not, it doesn't mean we are inferior either. We all live our lives, day by day, year by year, and experience things that arise for US. We do not have the same experience as anyone else, and nor do we think exactly the same way. So, if anyone judges our knowledge against their own, we need to feel strong and know that we might not know the world's knowledge the same as them, but we have our own unique knowledge and experiences of the same world, be it historical, from books, or from our own feelings.

Self-doubt – we all know it, but let's tell it where to go!

I was washing the dishes one morning a couple of years ago, and got thinking about college and how well I felt I did in my CBT role play the day before, when I got yet another pang of self-doubt about it. Can I do the course and become a counsellor?

Contradictory thoughts are pretty destructive as they frustrate, confuse and even anger the person having them. On this occasion, I felt none of those, because I immediately remembered that everyone gets some sort of nerves when beginning a new role, a new job, and a new life changing event occurs or any big change in their lives.

Then I remembered when I was a recruitment consultant for Manpower UK. I passed all the training with flying colours, was offered a role immediately and flourished in the role of interviewing job seekers and finding them jobs to go into, either permanent or temporary. Before I knew it I had a great little team of warehouse workers, manual workers and forklift drivers and lots of clients who gave me all their jobs to fill on first meeting. I had the gift. But, I still found myself driving the commute to work and occasionally having a surge of self-doubt run through my brain. I'd want to turn the car around and go home. I'd think about my job and try to picture myself in it and I couldn't. I felt as though I couldn't possibly do the job and couldn't even remember what it was that I was doing.

I never did turn round, and once I was in the office and the phones were ringing, my clients were coming in, and I checked my diary, I was too busy to worry anymore and just found myself doing the job.

The funny thing is that, even on day one, when I had no idea what I was doing, I remember the phone ringing and I just looked at it, hoping that the other lady in the office would answer it. I turned to the regional manager who was there to welcome me in my new job, and he just urged me to pick up the phone. And there I was answering it. "Good morning, Manpower, how can I help?"

And it just went from there. In at the deep end and I succeeded.

Self-doubt is there for all of us, but the great feelings that come from taking a challenge, making a life changing decision, or anything of that nature, far outweighs the negative feelings.

When feeling depressed or anxious, self-doubt often comes knocking at our door, so it is up to us to shake it off. I find writing down the predicament helpful. I look at the pros and cons of things, analysing just how much I REALLY believe my doubts, and most times the evidence is there that we have nothing much to doubt. We can then move on and get on.

And I know that I am a good counsellor; I thrive in learning new things, and I study well. So, next time Mr Self-doubt comes knocking at my door, I'm going to tell him to hop it, as usual: and quick!

A self-worth tip!

This is especially helpful if we experience self-destructive behaviours and low self-worth.

To find out how to look after yourself in the best way and to find out what you really think, if a matter arises that is negative, just ask yourself what you would tell your loved one to do if they were in the same predicament. We might not look after ourselves at times, but want the best for those close to us, and this is a great way to re-evaluate what we do ourselves.

Igniting memories for inspiration in life

I have a total of twenty-three pot plants and flowers outside the front of my house. I have no garden, just a driveway, but am making the most of it.

I planted some bright red geraniums in memory of my Great Aunt who played a loving and big part in my childhood until my twenties. I bought a black metal plant stick with a fork on the top and room to write a few words on white card under plastic. Not only did my Great Aunt cook the most delicious of foods for which she was adored, but she grew all her vegetables and fruit in her garden, so the 'fork' was apt for both!

My hamster died recently so I bought the brightest most floral hand painted pot I could find, and a bright pink Cyclamen and buried her in it. She was a lot of fun and really bright and playful, so this was an apt memorial for her.

Is there an important person from your life you can remember with flowers, plants, vegetables or fruit at your home?

Just be yourself today, let it all go and show others who you really are!

I was able to cry in front of mum and dad recently! We were watching a programme about animals – it was sad. I hid my tears for a bit, as I have for most of my life, and then I let go and let them flow even allowing mum and dad to notice. I had to go out of the room quite quickly, to wash my face, but at least I let them see.

I think they were warmed by it, as it showed them a part of my personality they probably didn't think existed, and I could hear them mentioning it as I left the room.

I am a nice, caring person, I just haven't always shown it with my hardened exterior or the way I muck about like a child. It has taken me a long time to realise it, as I have been very harsh on myself over the years, not even liking who I'd become most of the time, as I didn't know who I was and what I stood for in this life.

I do now; or at least I am getting there. I like myself now, and it shows in the way I look after myself; I am better with eating, body care and doing things I enjoy. I am very pleased indeed that I could cry that night, as I had spent my whole life since I was six years old covering up my many tears, partly, I believe, because my emotions were invalidated as a child and partly because I wanted to protect myself from showing my weaknesses.

Overcoming fears; socialising

Growing up, I was never a girl for hanging out in groups, bar a couple of times in junior school. Even then, the only reason I hung out in a group was to try to 'fit in' with everyone: even those who did and said things that I didn't agree with. I even found myself doing things I didn't agree with in order to fit in.

However, I was taught all kinds of subjects at school in classrooms full of children, I went to work and mixed with large groups of people - all types of personalities, many of which I wouldn't choose to socialise with, some who became good friends. I was fine with this, and even became supervisor and manager of many in various jobs, until…

My mental illness took over in a negative way.

Without going over that story, I became quite introvert in later years, finding myself paranoid, nervous and catastrophizing, at times, at the thought of mixing with people. I cancelled an outing with one of my brothers, missed a school reunion I wanted to go to, other social events and even evenings out with my boyfriend. It was a shame, but I preferred to hibernate than to mix.

The fact that I joined and finished my first Counselling college course three years ago was a big achievement; it got me out of the house, gave me a little regularity, and I learnt a subject I am very interested in. I even became good at the course and passed the exam.

So, in September 2013 I enrolled on the Counselling Skills level 2 course, and two of my friends from the first course were on it. I also began therapy for myself: group analytical psychotherapy. Apart from a few issues which led to a short absence from both group activities, I kept going. I knew that it would help me feel better and strengthen my mind if I continued.

I had disappointed myself too many times by talking myself out of experiences and social events, so I reminded myself each time a social opportunity came up too, and pushed myself to go. And I enjoyed myself.

A night out was arranged with my college friends. At first I felt really nervous and anxious; it was the whole group thing that made me nervous. I worried about what to wear, how I would behave, that I might drink too much due to nerves, that I might gamble too much (it was a meal at a casino), oh it went on…

Calm down, deep breaths…

I phoned one of my friends and arranged to meet her outside the casino so that helped. But my poor tummy was doing somersaults as my IBS was triggered by the stress, and I was very shaky - even though I knew it would be a good night.

And it was a lovely night. It was wonderful to see everyone – they are very lovely ladies. Only seven of us turned up out of fifteen, so it was a very manageable group for me too! I got into it very easily and had fun, but I was pretty excitable and didn't eat that much. I knew the fear was in my head and unfounded. I did drink, but I didn't get drunk. We all had a good laugh, chatting all night and I felt comfortable. I was pleased with myself. Up until then, I had lost my identity in a way. I had lost touch with who I was, acting in a way to try to fit in with varying people, but I certainly was 'just myself' on that night.

That was over a year ago and I continue to get better all the time.

I continued to draw on memories like those when I needed to find the confidence to get out and about. Now I just go without having to talk myself into it.

Group analysis – resentment, anger and depression

Every week in group analysis I heard shocking, sad, awful stories of true life events. Every week I could relate to many of my fellow patients' thoughts and feelings. Relating is good as it means I can empathise, but relating also meant it was a trigger factor for me. At one point when trying to convey my issues, I found myself feeling suddenly sick and ill, shaking and sobbing uncontrollably. It was hard to breathe in between sobs. I could hear everyone's concern for my welfare, but, for a few minutes, it was like I wasn't connected to anyone in the room. I knew something had been brewing because of the IBS and spasms in my belly from time to time. Occasionally, my breathing had been a little shallow, my concentration for reading had been poor and my dreams had been more and more nightmarish and scary. But despite these signs I was still shocked at my reaction.

This was another one of those times when I couldn't hide my tears – it was out of my control. I felt embarrassed and annoyed that it happened and that I may have looked like I was attention seeking, but I wasn't.

"We must keep ourselves in check all the time when it comes to mental illness"

Whilst counselling, some clients speak of how they do not feel 'real' and true to themselves. To keep the peace with family members or others, they endure criticism without argument. They cannot share their true feelings, thoughts and behaviours – they feel they need to put on an act. They feel like a child in the relationship, or inferior. I have had experiences with feeling like that in the past, so I can truly empathise and without sharing my personal experiences with clients, per say, I share my wisdom by way of questioning. I work with individuals to help them find their own way to be more assertive, using self-respect. I discuss with clients how many people have a persona for various situations, be it work, certain family members, events etc. We live in a social system that makes us that way. Not all of us, but many. We might be more polite at work, or speak better when with those who speak well, or say we are fine when we are not. We might want to prove ourselves to our parents if they are strict and have high expectations of us, we might tell family what we think they want to hear, we might find any way to please people…

We hide our inner pain. There is a place and time for everything, whether in sharing written words, conversations, photos, thoughts and feelings. I do not put on an act these days for anyone, and am true to myself and respect myself, although on-line I prefer to share positivity, contentment and inspiration; that is what social media is for, in my mind.

Let's move onto something really positive. Ask yourself "What makes me happy?"

Find some time to yourself, and have a good think, writing down everything you can think of that makes you happy. You don't have to do it in one go; just keep the list and add to it when you think of something else.

To get you going, here's some things that make me happy…

1. I love ALL animals - from seeing them on TV, to real life, to touching them, to interacting with them and to having them share my house with me, I love ALL animals and more than anything else, they cheer me up. They are innocent, pretty much, only kill to eat, pretty much, and virtually all of them do not play vicious games or mind games, or abuse one another. You get my drift. Our human destruction and abuse of animals greatly upsets and angers me, but animals bring me great joy. Number one!

2. Days out – from museums where I learn of history, to walks in the fresh air round beautiful gardens, to a wander round the shops with coffee, it is great to get out and about and make the most of life, one day at a time.

3. Travel – meeting people from different counties or countries, tasting various foods, taking different roads, and just a bit of adventure outside of my local area.

4. My mind can be a bit flighty in that I have 20 internet windows open, 4 word documents, and emails, all at the same time, but I learn so much on-line about various subjects. I also like to learn from books, museums etc but especially discussions where varying points of views are brought forward.

5. So I think 'discussions' should have a place of its own in this list, as it doesn't matter if it's with just one other person or a group, in person or on-line, learning from other people's points of view, ideas, or knowledge is great.

6. Massage! I would have a massage every day if I could. It's great for my back but also very relaxing! From Thai to Swedish, they're all good!

7. A nice haircut and blow dry – it's so lovely coming out of the salon with sleek, soft, freshly cut hair.

8. I just love my food; Thai, Japanese, Italian, Indian, Spanish, Mexican… so many kinds. I guess all my far flung travels

encouraged me to try new foods early on, and we are so lucky now as we can get so many different foods in the UK, to eat out or cook at home. I love British food too, and try to be mindful of flavour, smell and texture, as it's relaxing and means I enjoy my food even more! Indian cuisine is my comfort food.

9. Stroking my cats, Titus and Millie. They have to have their own listing, as they're gorgeous! I love to lay my head on them while they purr – it's hypnotic and very relaxing. They say that stroking a cat regularly lowers blood pressure too and helps our body release a relaxation hormone! :-)

10. Watching interesting documentaries and true life films. I love to escape into these, and thankfully, because I have my *freeview* recorder, I can watch things when I want to, and do not have to watch rubbish. Some days I don't have the TV on at all, but others, I just get embroiled in other people's lives. From murderers, to inspiring stories I find it all interesting.

11. This brings me to books. I don't read enough, but when I find a cracker of a book, that feeling of never wanting to put it

down and thinking about when I can pick it up again, is great!

12. Chatting to people about their lives – I just find other people's lives so interesting. It never ceases to amaze me what people have been through, how they have overcome difficulties, and how they keep themselves happy. I guess that is why I am a counsellor, as I have always been interested in others. Men and women have found it easy to talk to me about just about anything.

13. Having a nice day with my mum and dad :-)

14. Writing! Whether I am writing my personal journal, to make sense of my own life, college journals to log my learning progress, college essays that require pre-study, or a blog post or book; I love it all! And to publish them and share my words and thoughts with the world is great too.

15. This brings me to social media. OK I am on Facebook and Twitter FAR too much, but I do love it: chatting to people,

learning snippets of things and finding new books to read by fellow indie authors! Oh yes, and finding new blogs too! (Using #ArchiveDay on Saturdays and #SundayBlogShare on Sundays, #wwwblogs on Wednesdays and #MondayBlogs on Mondays, bloggers share their blog articles and there are some great ones)

16. Getting in bed once I have changed the bedding – crisp fresh sheets, duvet and pillows, mmm…

17. Music! Music ignites memories so songs can make me sad but generally they make me happy. I can be transported in my mind to my younger days of raving, to holidays, to special nights out… radio, ipod, CD, from pre-planned music to whatever comes on next, it's all good.

18. I love the quiet. I am lucky and live in a quiet area, and I like it that way. I like noise, but in smaller quantities these days…

19. Getting nice feedback or a good review for one of my books. Firstly, it excites me every time I know someone is reading

one of them, but to get feedback or a review, is even better. The same applies knowing that people are reading my blogs!

20. I love cuddles.

21. Knowing that people are there if I really need them.

22. Driving – especially at night when it's quiet on the roads and I have the radio on.

23. Remembering my three favourite words: individuality (because we are all individual – I have a tattoo of this in Japanese), spontaneity (just seeing what happens) and strength (because it's our inner strength that gets us through our lives and through adversities – I also have a tattoo of this in Japanese)

24. Overcoming challenges. 'Feel the fear, but carry on'. It's amazing what we can do if we expose ourselves to some

challenges. And the elation of overcoming challenges is awesome!

25. Knowing that I have helped or inspired someone - in any way.

26. Back to animals to finish off... Looking after my tropical fish and watching them. Anything to do with Titus, my cat, especially his snoring next to me whilst laying on his back with his paws in the air, and playing chase and catch! And getting to know my kitten, Millie, who is just lovely.

I could probably go on... I don't wish to bore you... But, the last three are...

- Going to college and studying counselling, with a lovely bunch of supportive people!

- Self-development and self-analysis, both through therapies, writing, college, counselling clients and self-help – basically learning about who I am now and who I was in the past. This helps me to further understand myself and others so I can make positive changes and become a better person.

- Flowers and gardening – love it!

Resilience

Resilience is our inner strength to deal with situations, feelings, thoughts and actions. We need it. And the way to get it, without being totally heartless, is to find balance in how we observe, feel about and treat others, and how we observe, feel about and treat ourselves. It really is a case of being good to yourself allows you to be good to others. If you hate yourself, you might feel bad about others. If you are self-critical you may criticise others' thinking that they are criticising you (called 'projection') If you feel comfortable with who you are, you will probably be balanced in how you feel about others.

If I find myself acting out self-destructive behaviours I keep it in check through self-reflection and self-analysis and can deal with it before it gets out of hand.

So, have a think today about how you feel about yourself and how that might affect the way you feel, behave or think about others. How are your self-reflection and self-analysis skills? Are you balanced? Do you like yourself? Love yourself? Enjoy your own company? Is there anything in your personality that you don't like? If there is, do you find yourself projecting that dislike onto others?

Life is far too stressful, fast paced and busy, so it can take a lot of effort to just stop and take stock but it truly is worth it, for yourself and for better interpersonal relationships.

C is for…

Cognitive Behavioural Therapy (CBT)

Bad stuff happens to everyone, but it is how we deal with problems that are different, since we are all individuals. The same event can manifest in anger, upset or simple indifference depending on the person. It's about perception. And I recommend you to look at your own life in this way too. It really does help you see yourself, even if what you see, you don't like that much.

Cognitive Behavioural Therapy is a structured psychological treatment. It aims to tackle everyday difficulties through problem-solving techniques, and encourages us to replace negative thinking patterns with positive ones. Dialectical behaviour therapy (DBT) was derived from CBT, but was updated to help people who really struggle particularly with self-harming behaviours.

Cognitive Behavioural Therapy (CBT) worked wonders for me whilst in the deepest depths of Obsessive Compulsive Disorder (OCD) and depression. I knew there were major issues surrounding my childhood, men and my behaviours and how I had become out of control at times and very self-destructive. CBT helped me to break down the process of bad behaviour, by understanding that a thought can create an emotion and depending upon the emotional make-up of an individual, this can create a bad behaviour. The idea is to break the thoughts that trigger an emotion which then triggers behaviour. Although in many cases this is a 'present' centred therapy, and does not delve into the past, it can be modified, taking into account previous experiences which may have influenced a person's fundamental beliefs. In my case, as it was necessary, we did look at the past. We worked on finding out what the core beliefs were for some of my very negative thinking about myself and others as I was so sensitive about others' negative comments aimed at me (or comments I 'believed' were aimed at me)

We also looked at the emotions that were triggered at differing times, such as fear, sadness, hate and resentment. I wrote journals of my thoughts, feelings and behaviours in different situations and used scaling questions to work out how bad things were out of a scale of ten, so that we could work on them to make them more positive experiences. We were also able to identify what my obsessions were, the compulsions they created in me and the outcomes.

For example, I would be convinced that the sun would shine through a glass left near a window and set fire to my flat (obsession) and I would have to go back to my flat to move the glass (compulsion). This, to me, was a very real and possible outcome (it was my reality), so we had to use systematic desensitization to get over such obsessions and the subsequent compulsions. In this case she asked me to go out, to not go back to check the door was locked (another compulsion of mine as I could never remember actually locking the door) and to leave the glass where it was, on the window sill. And through time, by doing this, I changed my thought process to the knowledge that when I got home I had locked the door and the flat had not burst into flames. We worked on many more, much worse, issues, but I got over many of them and we finished the therapy when I was ready, which was great as I didn't feel let down or that I was left with issues. We did not work on issues that could not be helped via CBT in any case, of which there were still many, but my anxiety, obsessions and depression had subsided well enough to be able to function properly. She suggested that it takes time to take on new skills like those, and that, in time, I would use them more and more in other situations as well. I did, and I am still using those skills learnt in many situations to date.

Here's an example from August 2007, when first introduced to the idea of CBT, that showed how I took simple incidents and looked at my own reactions to them.

I was invited to a wedding reception:

Activating event – I got tired of shopping for clothes and shoes for the wedding

Consequences – I was fed up & tired

Your actions – grumpy & pessimistic

Beliefs – I can't do my websites as I am doing everything for my boyfriend and his friend's wedding

Thinking error – It's not all for him, I am getting a new dress, bag and shoes.

Outcome – I cheered up & so had a better shop!

My CBT forms got a little more questioning –

This one is called the 'Daily Thought Record'

1. Situation –

    Who were you with?

    Where were you?

    What were you doing?

2. Negative Automatic thoughts

    Rate believability of thoughts (0-100%)

3. Rate Intensity of emotion (0-100%)

4. **Alternative and balanced thoughts**

   Rate believability of thoughts (0-100%)

5. **How do you feel now?**

   Re-rate intensity of emotions (0-100%)

It is apparently the core beliefs that set off emotional triggers when things happen, such as jealousy or aggravation so that's where you start.

We needed to get to the root of my issues, and we found that one of my core beliefs was the need to have attention/compliments/appreciation from others. It probably stemmed from my dad, who didn't come to parents' evenings at school, and who didn't know how hard I was working and what great marks I was getting. I have strived all my life to be appreciated by Dad. That became clear.

So we had one core belief that we could work on: fear of failure

We looked at the circle of CBT which is that a thought sets off an emotion which sparks a reaction (action) and that action sets off a thought, which sets off an emotion - hence a repeating cycle.

So, she wrote down an example. My boyfriend had a 'separate' life (friends/family) he didn't want me to be a part of, for reasons only he knew, but for me it was terribly upsetting as I had never been excluded from family and friends of a long term boyfriend in the past…

Thought –

- I am being excluded from my boyfriend's life

- I am not worthy of meeting his step grandchildren and family and friends (He didn't want me to)

-

Emotion –

- Angry

- Depressed

Action –

- Argue

Then, we discussed how much worse, mentally, these issues with him and his family made me feel. She told me:

> ***Feeling ill makes me angry/depressed, and makes me argue with my boyfriend***

> ***We cannot change our emotions, only our thoughts and actions***

But how?

I had to think myself worthy of his love and change my actions to something more positive. I said that I had unearthed my exercise/yoga videos and could do one of them for relaxation. I also could do some more of my positive working ideas, such as promoting my aerial photos to local newspapers etc.

Thought pattern

Situation – Chris went to visit his family and he didn't invite me

Thoughts - I am excluded. I am not good enough to be part of his life

Body/physical sensations – stomach problems/spasms/IBS

Moods and emotions – anger, depression

Thoughts – you make me ill/you don't care

Behaviours – what I did/didn't do – I have an argument with Chris

And it goes round again

Circle of thoughts – event, thoughts, feelings, behaviours, events, thoughts, feelings, behaviours...

Dr Lamb was pleased when I said I was moving out of my boyfriends (it was not going well at the time) into a place on my own, as she said that I would prove to myself that I could make it on my own, look after myself, keep myself company and be fine. We worked out what my main core beliefs that got in the way of my happiness and life were.

I wrote down my Core beliefs

About myself:

I am not able to cope on my own

I need others to feel OK

I am a failure/not good enough/worthless

I have no self esteem

About others:

People are judgemental

People are not supportive/lack understanding

Men should not be trusted/will use me

So, taking the beliefs about *myself*, I had made these assumptions and rules:

- I need other peoples' attention to feel good about myself
- Other people must show me attention at all times
- If I don't get other peoples' attention/approval, then this means that I have failed/am not good enough
- It is horrible/awful when I don't get other peoples' attention/approval
- I can't cope on my own, I need other people to support me
- If I make mistakes, then this means that I have failed.

Thinking 'I can't cope on my own'

- Caused anxiety = confirming to myself that I was right, I *can't* cope on my own
- I stayed in the relationship and relied on Chris - for practical and emotional issues = confirming to myself that I can't cope on my own

- I would stay in negative situations

Thinking 'I am unworthy'

- Made me become needy
- Caused even lower self esteem
- Led to thoughts of being a failure
- Made me resort to self-destructive behaviour as punishment

These thoughts lead to:

- Low self esteem
- Neediness and feeling abandoned
- Lack of trust
- Choosing the wrong men – saying no to nice ones and choosing the bad ones and going back for more

Through CBT I learnt to challenge those thoughts, for example:

'I can't cope on my own – I need people to be happy'

We logged various thoughts, behaviours and outcomes throughout the therapy and we looked back to find evidence that I CAN cope on my own; there were lots of examples of when I did.

Gradually, logging all this evidence that I was getting better convinced me that I WAS getting better, and highlighted continuing proof that I was overcoming one core belief, one action, one thought, at a time.

I moved out on the 14th February 2011– Valentine's Day.

I logged some of my thoughts:

Event – woke up to realise how much I have got to do to pack up and leave and set up my new home

Thoughts and images – me getting stressed, it's all happening because of my boyfriend and his thoughts about his family

Moods/emotions – anger and stress started and low mood – fed up

Behaviours/what I did or didn't do – got really annoyed, blaming him, feeling hateful and telling him we'd never stay friends now that he has chosen his feelings for his ex-wife over feelings for me and has made me leave his flat.

Body/physical sensations – angry, uptight, stressed and tense.

Thoughts/images – He doesn't care (because he is ignoring what I am saying), he cares only about his ex-wife, family and himself, I hate him.

By the 17th February just three days later, I was so stressed Dr Lamb noticed I wasn't myself. I felt strange and dissociated. Stress was the cause. I was worrying about being alone in my flat – being abandoned. Could I cope? I got to my appointment because I couldn't miss it, but I couldn't remember driving there. I felt empty. It was like my head was in a TV or something, and I was looking out, through a tunnel, but not really present in the world that I was looking out onto; a surreal feeling. I was going through the motions with my body and mouth, and I could see what was happening in my immediate surroundings, but at the same time I wasn't noticing, I couldn't really *see*. It was like a mild psychosis due to stress and depression, and it wasn't the first time I had experienced it, but it was the first time I had been out of the house and experienced it. Luckily Dr Lamb encouraged me to talk and coaxed me back into the real world.

She encouraged me to get out and not stay in the flat on my own, hibernating and drinking which I was so prone to doing. She wrote out a pros and cons for it:

Stay at home

- Even if I stay at home all day (in my comfort zone) I will have more chances to worry about things and drink

- Staying at home makes me feel low; I think about the past and I end up drinking alcohol

Go out

- I will be pleased and proud of myself for achieving things

- If I am pleased and proud of myself then I will feel less depressed

- If I know I have to go out then I work harder, and I am more productive

- I will not drink and this will help me feel less depressed

- I will break my self-destructive patterns and I will weaken my self-destructive beliefs

- In the past when I didn't listen to my self-destructive urges, I did something constructive and I felt good about it

Journal: March 2011

Dr Lamb– what we have achieved so far…

- *I have found out what my core beliefs are (that I am a failure, I have no self-esteem, that men are horrible and I have to affirm this by my negative actions which will make people not like me, make me have unstable relationships, and drink alcohol as a self-harm behaviour and don't look after myself) so I could overcome those core beliefs*
- *I have overcome loneliness*
- *I have found more motivation to go out*
- *I am overcoming being late and understanding why I am late (time management)*
- *I understand the circle of how an event triggers a belief, which triggers a reaction and I recognise how I should have dealt with it, so that I can learn how to stop bad reactions and outcomes occurring.*
- *I take responsibility for myself without being scared.*

- *If I enter a depressive episode, I can recognise it and do not give into it – I can stop and take action before I spiral out of control.*

It is clear to me that I have been overcoming depression and that is a big step; I have overcome a lot of negative symptoms and the control I gain gives me less symptoms to work on, and gradually I will kick them all in the butt.

A Women's Magazine asked me to tell my story; the focus was my depression. I said yes, with no worries about rejection which was a big step in the right direction. They visited my flat to do my make-up and a photo shoot and the article was really good!

Appointments: To tackle my constant lateness, I kept a diary of times I had to attend an appointment whether with Dr Lamb, the dentist, doctors, hairdressers, and reasons why I was or was not late. I used blank hour by hour diaries, which Dr Lamb supplied so I could plan my hours/days/weeks better. My mission was to stay busy but also find time to relax – keep a few gaps. Thing was, I kept doing so many other things in trying to go out and do nice things, I began to feel stressed that I wasn't working enough on my book and websites at home, so I logged my work hours on the diaries too.

I like having my own space and am getting used to the idea of it

When I told Dr Lamb, "I've been given anti-depressants, I'm not better!" she said "You are generalising. You have made lots of progress and changes for the better. You cannot say that you are not better. The doctor probably gave them to you for the short term to help you cope with your current situation." Of course, what I didn't realise was that anti-depressants can be very helpful for the anxiety side of depression and extremely helpful for anxiety driven OCD traits. I still thought depression was just about being sad and suicidal and feeling useless.

We looked for evidence of me *getting worse*, but it was clear **I was getting better**. I was. What I didn't want was to be doing my photo shoot for my story on getting over depression and thinking the whole time I was lying and a fake that I was better when I wasn't, but **I WAS better.** It took up quite a lot of the appointment, but Dr Lamb went over many concepts that we had worked out from the past, as I was in overdrive, talking and worrying about getting angry with various people, and she said to do a pros and cons list for getting angry with them, to see if I am right to get annoyed and whether it was worth it.

I told her I still had black and white thinking. So we went through a thoughts form together and we could find no reason to feel depressed about the medications. I was not suicidal, I was getting out and about. I had more-or-less finished my book. She said that I did not have schizophrenia and I did not have psychotic depression either, which is where a patient goes into catatonic states and often needs ECT (Electro-Convulsive Treatment) to get them out of it. I wasn't my mum. I WAS ME. AND I WAS GETTING BETTER AT BEING ME. I decided to stop looking at online forums, labels and symptoms as I was slotting myself into all sorts of diagnoses, but was wrong. One must NEVER self-diagnose a mental disorder; it must always be done by a professional in the field.

I then used more detailed forms to help me:

Situation – who were you with? What were you doing? When was it? Where were you?

1. **Moods – describe each mood in one word. Rate the intensity of each mood (0-100%)**

2. **Automatic thoughts – what was going through my mind just before I started to feel this way? What does this say about me? What does this mean about me? My life? My future? What am I afraid might happen? What is the worst thing that could happen if this is true? What does this mean about how others think/feel about me? What images or memories do I have in this situation?**

3. Evidence that supports the HOT thought – circle the hot thought in the previous column for which you are looking for evidence. Write factual evidence to support this conclusion. (Try to avoid mind reading and interpretation of facts)

4. Evidence that does not support the HOT thought. Ask yourself questions to help discover evidence which does not support your HOT thought.

5. Alternative/balanced thoughts – ask yourself questions to generate alternative or balanced thoughts. Write an alternative or balanced thought. Rate how much you believe in each alternative or balanced thought (0-100%)

6. Rate mood now – copy the feelings from the second column. Re-rate the intensity of each feeling from 0 – 100% as well as any new records.

And to tackle obsessions, I was advised by Dr Lamb to challenge them. DON'T go back and check the hairdryer or oven. DON'T give in to the paranoia. Once I realised that the house didn't catch fire or something bad didn't happen, my thinking adjusted after time and I gave the obsession up, naturally. But, the act of continuously going back to check is like telling my brain that I am right to have the obsession surrounding the dangers, right to have the compulsion to go back and check and so, by habit, the automatic fears will continue. I had to write down the 'HOT' thought (the obsession/belief) and write what evidence I had to support it and I couldn't find any. There was no way the oven could turn on by itself. There was no way the glass could catch fire on the windowsill…

Dr Lamb also gave me a handout on depression so that I could understand it more fully. From it, I worked out what was relevant to me. It gave me a guide of signs to look out for when entering or in a depressive episode. It talked of catastrophizing where a person feels that 'everything' is going wrong, when it is not. Often a problem can be small but can be viewed as huge. It explained how physical fitness and energy levels can be affected by depression as well as the ability to concentrate and/or sleep. Also how a person's interest in sex can be affected. I could relate to all of these and more, but since I have talked about depression and the symptoms in detail in the introduction of this book, I will not re-list them all here.

Outcomes of CBT:

I was no longer getting as depressed.

I was no longer feeling quite so tired in the mornings from the medications.

I was feeling more positive.

I was no longer feeling paranoid.

I was ready to be on my own.

So, I have explained how CBT has helped me, but of course it is tailored to the individual. Could it help you?

D is for…

Doctors

I will not say too much about this subject, as it is down to an individual if they want to see their doctor about their issues, and there are good and bad doctors around. However, I will just say that it is worth considering. My personal experiences with GP's and Psychiatrists have been both good and bad, I have been against and for anti-depressants and anti-psychotics, and I have had good and bad therapies offered through the NHS, but it would be unfair to write about those experiences here.

Medical treatments

Anti-depressants – They work on the chemical messengers in ones' brain to lift ones' mood. They are not a cure, but offer to help with symptoms enough to allow the patient to deal with their depression more easily. There can be side effects, they do not work for everyone, and coming off them has to be slow as they can cause withdrawal symptoms. It is recommended to take them for at least six months and they begin to work between two and four weeks after the start of a course.

Electroconvulsive therapy (ECT) – I know little about this therapy, but the electrical process (electrical current through the brain) is administered whilst under general anaesthetic producing a convulsion to overcome very severe depression and psychosis.

There are many other ways to recover and I would suggest that the first place to go is to your GP who can offer medications or offer referrals to relevant services.

E is for…

Express yourself with your look

This is all about how you look -- to yourself and others. It's about building self-respect by being clean, groomed and clothed in whatever way suits you. Taking a little time on our appearance is a good thing. I am not talking about standing in front of the mirror saying mantras or spending hours transforming yourself (although there's nothing wrong with either of those), but I am just talking about not letting yourself go.

When I was in my darkest days I didn't care how I looked at times. If I stayed indoors for days, I might not wash for two or even three. Once I got into the habit of getting up, washing and dressing every day, I felt a whole lot better. I no longer had to cower if the doorbell rang, worried about being seen in a state. I could go out at the drop of a hat because I was ready. I could look in the mirror and be pleased with what I saw rather than repulsed by my lack of care.

You might have a certain fashion you like or specific style of your own, but in any case 'Take care of your appearance; making the effort will help no end'.

F is for…

Friends and family

Having support around you is important. You don't choose your family, but you can choose your friends, so do try to ensure that you are hanging out and communicating with people who are good for you. Negativity, jealousy, backstabbing, two faced, dismissive… are all warning signs for friends who aren't really friends. If you wanted to talk about your issues, could you? Would you be supported by your friends or would your issues be dismissed? Would you be told to get on with it, or would they talk about themselves instead? Ask yourself some questions to ensure you get the best from friends, and of course, that you try to offer them the same back.

If you are a friend or relative of someone suffering with depression and/or anxiety, then be there for them, don't shy away or be ignorant. Try to learn about how your friend/relative feels, and learn about ways you can help. Everyone likes to be listened to and sometimes that is all someone needs – not advice and not comments like 'get on with it'. If you are not asked for an opinion or advice, then either don't give it, or ask if they would like it. As a sufferer I know how hard it is when I try to tell someone about my issues, and they just show me or tell me what they think. I often do not speak because I do not want advice; I just want to vent or be heard.

G is for…

Get out

Days out can be great for the mind, body, soul, stress and depression

If I get myself out and about I often feel pretty good. My mind is clearer and my body--aches are not as prevalent. Sometimes, I can be out and about, granted, and still feel 'down', but most times it is an antidote to stress and depression for me.

I love to go to historic sites, museums, seeing animals, the seaside, countryside, the cinema, shops, restaurants and lots more. And when I do, I feel mentally refreshed, having concentrated on my five senses, (sight, sound, taste, touch and smell, known to help 'keep you in the moment') whilst taking in the environments and people around me, eaten nice food and taken much needed exercise. I feel tired sometimes if it's vigorous, but it's a nice tired.

Getting out and about doesn't cure depression and stress, but it sure can help to make some plans, even if it's just a walk in the countryside or a visit to a seafront, especially when the sun is shining. It may just make you feel better too if you are feeling low, and even if it is only temporary happiness and relief it's got to be better than none at all!

It is important that we take a break sometimes from our normal lives, even if just for a day, to refresh our minds, body and soul.

I tend to 'Live for Today!' too. I know responsibility takes over at times, and my mental health distress took away all those optimistic and positive feelings for a while, but now they are back and I do, every day, wake up and appreciate that I am still here and able to do things that I enjoy.

H is for…

Hobbies

This ties in with my 'relaxation' chapter, but hobbies do not necessarily have to be relaxing, especially if you like adrenalin sports such as skydiving or bungie jumping or other 'exciting' pursuits.

Adrenalin production is good if you work it off physically, but if you don't, it can transform into a mood changer – feelings of depression or anger or anxiety for example. That is why they call it 'fight or flight' when you are hit by adrenalin – will you fight the adrenalin off or stay still and let it build up inside of you creating bad moods…

Here are just a few hobbies I can think of:

Sewing

Knitting

Drawing/painting

Cooking

Walking/swimming

Quizzes/crosswords

Film or theatre

Sailing

Climbing

Music

TV

Reading

Writing

Volunteering

The list is endless, and it depends on an individual's preferences, but hobbies can be done alone, with others, for others, or out in the community. Helping in the community can be helpful in combatting any social issues you may have because of depression and anxiety; helping you to feel a part of something again, and make new friends or meet people with similar issues to your own.

    Participating in hobbies can broaden your knowledge and give you a sense of production, worth and wellbeing.

    Making a home for myself, tending to my potted plants and flowers, looking after my tropical fish and gorgeous cats, and taking a little responsibility for my parents in taking them out at least once a week, is doing wonders for my mental health. At eighty-one and eighty-four, they need help at times, and although they are not a 'hobby' it still gives a similar outcome for me – feeling better in myself.

I is for…

I can…

Short and sweet this one! Just say "I can!" whenever you doubt yourself. If you think about all the things you have overcome in your life that have been thrown at you thus far, you just know that you can deal with a whole lot more and that you are becoming more resilient every day. Of course some things simply cannot be done if they are out of our power, but I am talking about the things you can do – namely, you can help yourself to feel better!

J is for…

Jealousy

Jealousy – there's nothing nice about it. Not for the jealous person, nor for the recipient.

I have been jealous. I have felt the rage wanting to erupt from my insides. I have even been incapable of covering it up with some people in my past. It has wrecked friendships and made me look completely self-centred. But then, I probably was at the time.

However, it occurred to me a year ago that I no longer suffer with the green eyed monster bubbling away inside of my being. Why? Well, I had to think about that a little, and discuss it too, to clarify my thoughts…

Having dealt with many of my inner demons of mood swings, depression, anger, resentment and more, I began working on self-esteem and confidence. I do not mean not the type of confidence that would make me big headed, I talk of the confidence to be who I am, respect myself for who I am, and to trust myself again. I have managed a lot of that. And it seems that, without even realising it, any jealousy I had has gone by the by along with my self-resenting, self-destructive self.

So, it seems to me, that in my case, my jealousy came about because I wasn't happy in my own skin. My jealousy may have risen because someone was going on holiday, having good luck or falling in love, for example, and the pang of jealousy which of course at times led to guilt (another horrid feeling) could be crushing. But in actual fact, it wasn't the things they had or were going to do that I was jealous of really – it was the fact that those thing made them happy, because the person, in my eyes, was indeed happy. I was, I believe, actually jealous of their happiness.

I could have had the holiday, the good luck, the love, but it wouldn't have worked for me, as I wasn't in the right place in my head for those things to make me happy. I have been on holidays where I have been internally miserable. I have been shown love and it hasn't permeated to my heart. I have had good luck, but it gave me only short term enjoyment.

I NEEDED TO MAKE MYSELF HAPPY by being comfortable with 'myself' as a person, and thus allowing others to be more comfortable with me.

I needed to stop blaming everything and everyone, but myself, for how I felt.

I needed to stop blaming everything and everyone, but myself, for how things went wrong (even if it was just my perception of the event)

I needed to take ownership of my own freedom to change.

I needed to come out of denial that everything and everyone were to blame for my unhappiness, but me… Because the only thing I could change was me – not other people, nor events. It was how I reacted to, felt about, and accepted others and my problems that would get me out of the turmoil of blame, unhappiness and lack of self-worth and identity.

I have, over the past few years, tackled these issues, and am at peace with myself, and able to self-analyse naturally. This is great of course, since I am now a practising counsellor, but it will never stop. It is important to keep a close eye on myself, to ensure I am doing my best as a counsellor.

I am no longer jealous of anyone or anything, as far as I know…

It was a wonderful feeling, when on holiday, I made this realisation whilst driving along, relaxed, and was another reminder of how all my hard work to sort myself out and recover from my internal issues, was worth it.

And I didn't even need to tackle jealousy as a side issue – sorting out my inner self fixed that problem without me even realising.

When people are having good luck, are going on holiday, have something new that I might like myself, or are feeling really happy, I am, without even thinking about it, just very happy for them.

    That is a nice place to be.

K is for…

Knowledge

I am not a fan of 'labels' for people – Bipolar, Schizophrenic etc – because I feel each person is an individual and should not be put in a box full of symptoms. However, a diagnosis (if the right one is made) can help the person and their loved ones to read about and learn about the illness they have; the symptoms, ways to help or cope, and the prognosis.

I feel there is a fine line. When I found out I had Borderline Personality Disorder, for example, as one of my diagnoses, I read about it and talked to people on-line about it, and when looking at the prognosis, it looked very grim. I was then hounded with thoughts that I would never feel better; that my life was always going to be tormented by my mood swings. My Psychiatrist at the time didn't help either, as he felt the same and even warned my boyfriend of the trouble ahead that I would cause.

I have read similar things about depression and I am glad that I found the strength to look past my research and look deep into myself. Instead of concentrating on the diagnostic labels I had been given by psychiatrists and GP's, I wrote down ALL the things about me (how I felt, behaved, reacted) that were negative in my life. Basically I was looking for all the things I did not like about myself and analysed why I didn't like them and what they were. I then had a list of over fifty negative symptoms/thoughts/feelings/actions that needed to be changed. I also wrote things I did like about myself to avoid feeling completely negative!

Having realised that I cannot change other people, but only myself, and that I had to change myself as no-one else could, I came out of denial. I had been blaming everything and everyone else for my problems, finding ways to make it their fault and not mine. I stepped up and looked at things in proportion; taking a good look at what part I played in my own misery. I then took responsibility for myself and put those negatives in order of priority, so that the worst, most negative things were at the top of the list, the least negative or least important at the bottom of the list.

And then I ploughed through them, slowly but surely, concentrating on one thing at a time, and reversed everything I could from a negative to a positive. I had various talking therapies, tried medications, I read about ways of coping and I changed myself.

Now I do not want to over simplify here what was a long, and at times, tortuous journey and struggle, but I also cannot write all about it here as it would take too long. Indeed, I wrote two memoirs in order to get it all in!

Some on-line forums or other social media can be valuable for getting information and hearing about other people's stories, which can help us to feel less alone. However, we must be wary, as sometimes people write very triggering, upsetting things as well as focussed, helpful information and experiences. In my own experience, when clouded with mental illness, these ways didn't work for me as I kept coming across negativity and 'woe is me' attitudes which I was trying to stop in myself. I needed to stay as positive as I could muster, so in order to read other people's stories, I read memoirs of fellow sufferers. These were more balanced and all had a beginning, middle and end, so I got a rounded view, usually ending with positivity. Knowing that I was not alone with symptoms that made me feel so very alone and isolated, worked wonders for me.

I went to trusted websites on-line such as MIND, NHS and Rethink, and found helpful leaflets and guides to help me. I bought self-help books as well, so I would get a varied and interesting amount of information to help me.

A few years later, and I am now doing very well. If I do get depressed, I now know it will not last long as I can take back control fairly quickly.

So all I am saying is that knowledge is important, but being careful where we get the knowledge from is just as important.

L is for…

Lethargy, headaches and other physical symptoms you can overcome

Let's face it, the mental and physical symptoms of depression and anxiety can be quite cyclic. When we feel extremely down we may not move as freely, leading to aches and pains around the joints, neck and back. We may not drink enough water, leading to dehydration, which could cause lethargy, headaches and bowel movement issues. We may not eat properly, leading to hunger stress, stomach aches, lack of energy… You get the picture.

But of course, all these things can lead back to a low mood, thus prolonging the depressive stage; no wonder if we are tired, dehydrated, hungry and stressed.

Irritable bowel syndrome is linked to stress (my IBS definitely flares up if I am stressed or not eating properly).

Eating disorders can co-occur as self-punishment, obsession or a habit, causing weight, energy and vitamin deficiency issues. I was diagnosed with IBS, at age sixteen, after bingeing/starving/over-exercising as I had ruined my stomach and bowel regularity.

I have an underactive thyroid (hypothyroidism) which is linked to depression. It took over a year to work out what was wrong but once I was diagnosed by my GP through a simple blood test, I was given thyroxine to take for life. Although it helps a bit, I still suffer lethargy, as nothing is as good as your thyroid glands working properly themselves (they create a hormone that controls metabolism and the production of energy from foodstuffs we eat). It may well be worth getting a blood test done just in case…

Relaxation (see my chapter on this), eating well (and regularly), drinking plenty of water and doing some exercise can do wonders for energy levels and a depressed mood. I always prefer to seek professional help as I strongly believe in prevention against cure, but in any case, it has to be best to get a medical opinion.

M is for...

Mindful use of the senses

One of the basics of being mindful is simple – Live 'in the moment'.

Let's face it how can you enjoy life right now if you are always thinking about problems in the past or problems that might occur in the future?

How many of us totally enjoy this very moment? Not enough, I'd say.

If you are aware of your surroundings and senses fully in the moment, then you will feel more relaxed, more at peace, more fulfilled and more real. Awareness is great for anyone, but can also be very helpful for beating the symptoms of depression, anxiety, stress, BPD, OCD and other mental distractions. Mindfulness is a very powerful practice and using your senses is part of that.

Just think about your five special senses:

•Sight – look at photos, beautiful pictures, go out and see lovely scenery – be totally aware of the colours, shapes, patterns, darkness, brightness…

•Sound – listen and I mean really listen, and you will hear sounds you would not normally pick up; that tiny bird singing in a tree nearby, a child's voice… It could be anything or nothing. Maybe you will find yourself in complete silence, but for most of us this isn't the case. Be totally aware of any noises.

•Touch – I love different textures, from my soft furry cats to screwed up paper when I am having a clear out (I love clear outs too!). From relaxing to stimulating, our sense of touch can be as ignored as the rest of our senses but being aware can even make washing up a more relaxing thing to do; warm water, bubbles…

•Smell – For uplifting, there's coffee, cakes baking, flowers like roses and maybe even fried onions, but for relaxing, how about a walk in the fresh country air, or cut grass, dewy morning air, lavender oil… There are scents all around you.

•Taste – this has to be my favourite way to get myself back 'in the moment' especially in the past when I would feel slightly 'out of the real world'. These are never ending – two of my personal favourites are strong flavours like curry (comforting) and coffee (stimulating), but I like to practise eating and taking in every flavour so that I can work out the recipe – herbs, onions, spices – a bit like the contestants have to do on *Masterchef*. It's a great way to really enjoy your food and appreciate the wonderful sense of taste we are blessed with.

You can do this at any time – stuck in a traffic jam, at home combined with awareness of your breathing as a kind of mindful meditation, whenever you feel you could do with this easy coping skill. It could just be a few minutes, or half hour, but when you reap the benefits, you can decide for yourself how often you want to practise it.

Sometimes I sit and contemplate what I can remember from the last week in terms of sight, sound, smell, taste and touch. It helps me to be in touch with recent goings on, and helps my memory so maybe it will work for you. It can be great writing therapy and tool too if I write it all down.

Some of mine a few months back…

Sight – aerial views out of the aeroplane window, beautiful Cambridge, crowds of people in shorts and dresses, ice cream melting down the cone, sun and blue skies, my cat, hamster and fish, Michael's face and hair, rain, lightening, clouds, mum's blue eyes crying, the injury on her head, elderly residents in care homes, frail, disabled and sad looking or smiling, care workers laughing with kind faces, green trees and beautiful flowers of all colours…

Sound – the hum of the aeroplane, people speaking across the radio into my headphones, an elderly woman shouting 'help!' over and over in the care home my mum is now living in, birds singing outside my bedroom window, the dustbin cart and crashing of bins being emptied, flies buzzing in the house (ugh!), Titus purring rhythmically, music and chatter on the radio, tv programmes, hairdryers and chatter in the hairdressers, buzzing electrical instruments in the dentist, car horns, alarm clock, cooking timer, mum crying, mum telling me she prefers my hair blonde…

Smell – Urine and air freshener in care homes, musty old smells, obnoxious effluvia's, baked potatoes, smelly bins in the heat, the fresh smell Titus brings in from outside in his fur, Indian food, garlic, deodorant, fish and chips…

Taste – fish and chips with salt and vinegar, creamy ice creams, lemonade, garlic bread, salmon and cucumber sandwiches…

Touch – My cat's soft fur, my kitten's even softer fur, Titus walking over me in bed to wake me up, heat!!! My fan blowing a breeze at me, the air conditioning in my car, wind blowing through the car with the windows down, sweaty body, aching back, aching ankles and feet, headaches, my hair being washed and massaged, cold water showering over my body, a hot hairdryer on my head, kissing mum's little face, a cuddle of mum's tiny body, soft pillows on mum's care home bed…

See how much can you remember from the past week. At the end of this chapter, you will find my six-day challenge to de-stressing with using your senses mindfully.

A ditty, poem, rhyming verse, whatever you want to call it, that I made up about mindfulness and living in the moment in 2015…

Stressed to my hilt, about my parents' health and care

I went to Portugal with my boyfriend, and I managed to chill out there

For the first time, in many years, I left all my troubles behind

As I practised relaxation skills, it's about 'training of your mind'

'Being in the moment' is somewhere many of us are not at

We like our technology, a fast paced life, materialism and all that

Mobile phones, we can't stop texting, telly on while we try to eat

It's no wonder we don't think constructively, so many challenges we must meet

But, it doesn't have to be like this, if we just took a little time out

To enjoy this moment, right here and now, without our problems, anger or doubt

Smell the coffee, the fresh cut grass, the beautiful blossom on the trees

Feel the sunshine, the soft fresh bedding, or cool sensation from the breeze

The taste of dinner, a fresh fruit salad, a warm hot chocolate or breakfast tea

Hear the birds they are all tweeting, or just pure silence is good for me

I see the beauty of the landscape, humans, animals and their pets

And as my brain soaks all these things up, the more relaxed my body gets

For I cannot concentrate on all those pleasures, and still be contemplating my woes

If you try it, you could be like me, and be calm from your head to toes

We spend far too much time worrying about what might happen, what has happened, and all our problems that we can often forget to live for today. We only get one life, and it is relatively short, so to live much of it in the past or the future is futile. There's a lot more to 'living today' of course, such as forgiveness, coping mechanisms, patience, not being greedy, not being jealous and so much more, but being mindful is a great place to start. It is almost like giving the mind a little holiday and that is often what we need in order to appreciate our lives, find the solutions we need that we often cannot due to over thinking, and it is one of our paths to better health.

When I came back from a holiday, stress hit me again, very hard, but two days later, I wrote it all down, prioritised, analysed, and found ways to see my problems in perspective. And I was OK again. It does require practise.

Mindfulness – never under-estimate it!

So, next time you are late driving somewhere, on a train or a bus, forget worrying about what might happen when you get there, or regretting not leaving earlier, or getting angry at the reason for the delay… Just be in the moment.

Wind down the window, listen for birds, sounds, smells… Look around you; what is going on… If there's nothing you can do about being late, just calm down and enjoy those extra few minutes…

When you are eating, really enjoy each mouthful instead of stuffing it in whilst watching TV and then realising, afterwards, that you hadn't even taken much notice of your dinner.

When you walk along a high street or through a park, take notice of other people, animals, nature; looking at the floor won't make your life more pleasant but integrating with the world around you might.

And even if you are looking forward to finishing work or towards a holiday, don't wish your life away – grasp every minute of it. Life will not wait for you.

One last note: let's face it, if that horrible thing you've convinced yourself about hasn't happened yet, and you haven't got it in writing, then there's a good chance it won't happen at all.

Culture

In traditional cultures, the focus is on the 'here and now' and the 'past'. In Western cultures, the focus is on the 'future'. It is no wonder, then, that I take from the Buddhist culture (mindfulness) and the Hindu culture (yoga) to help me to focus on the present and enjoy it before it is made history!

I didn't even realise it until I began my research, but I am quite spiritual and take from other cultures in that way (plus 'Fate' from the Hindu 'Karma' idea and a desire to do things at my own pace without making appointments/living my life by time constraints) in order to find some balance in this crazy, fast paced

Western World. It's a contradiction, though, as we counsellor's counsel clients to help them take control of their lives, moods, behaviours, which is the western way, yet 'fate' is all about things happening without our input as an individual…

Although I am involved in it, materialism is something I dislike, as well as our excessive need for fast progress, tainting our history very quickly with the terms 'old fashioned' etc.

Gardening is soothing, a responsibility, a stress reliever, gives a sense of production and the sight and smell of flowers is wonderful for the mind – my potted plant garden

I do not have a garden, sadly, but I do have a driveway area the front of my house and, apart from my car, I have a mixture of twenty odd pots close to the house door and wall. I began building my collection when I first moved in and felt like settling down, in mind and body, as my mental health issues were reducing.

Since then, my pets and my pot garden have been two of my best sources for de-stressing, as well as wonderful days out and learning and experiencing new things, which I also write about. All are simple things really; we can give a home to pets that suit our abilities and who need little or a lot of care, we can build gardens that need little or much care, and we can take days out that require little or much money or effort. It's our choice, but there's a choice for everyone.

I began setting up my pot garden last year when I moved into my little house and to see things popping up that I never expected to repeatedly grow and flower from last year is amazing. I have since added seedlings and ready to go plants to my pot collection, and it gives me great pleasure to observe them growing and flowering, or to water them and move them around depending on what colours go best together. Titus and Millie love to hang out with me while I potter too.

Watching my plants and flowers grow and change gives me a sense of pride and when my daffodils came out I snipped them off and brought them indoors to enjoy them even more.

I hope that you like gardening too and enjoy the outdoors. If you don't then there's no reason not to – you don't need a garden, just a little space to grow things in pots, but I could almost guarantee it will brighten your life to grow something, whether it be herbs, vegetables, flowers, plants or trees!

Whether you have holidays, days out, do gardening, go to therapy, adopt or foster a new pet, or any other of things I do for my well-being, I hope it works for you – enjoy your life NOW!

So here we finally at my 'Six days to simple mindfulness and better contentment' (if you are blessed with all five senses use them and if not, use all those that you do have)

Day one - all about sight

I want you to think about everything that you 'see' today (obviously if you are blessed with the sense of sight) Our minds take in so much on a day to day basis, it's incredible, but I am talking about what you 'really' see, not just what your sub conscious sees.

    I, like everyone, spend much time in thought; busy working out what I'm doing next, or what has happened, or what might happen, that it takes me away from the present moment. And to really 'live our lives' not just exist in them, we need to be 'in the now' not the past or the future (although obviously we cannot do it all the time and we do need to plan, that is a different matter)

So, everywhere you go today, have a good look around, whether it's at:

- Blue skies

- Sunshine

- Buildings

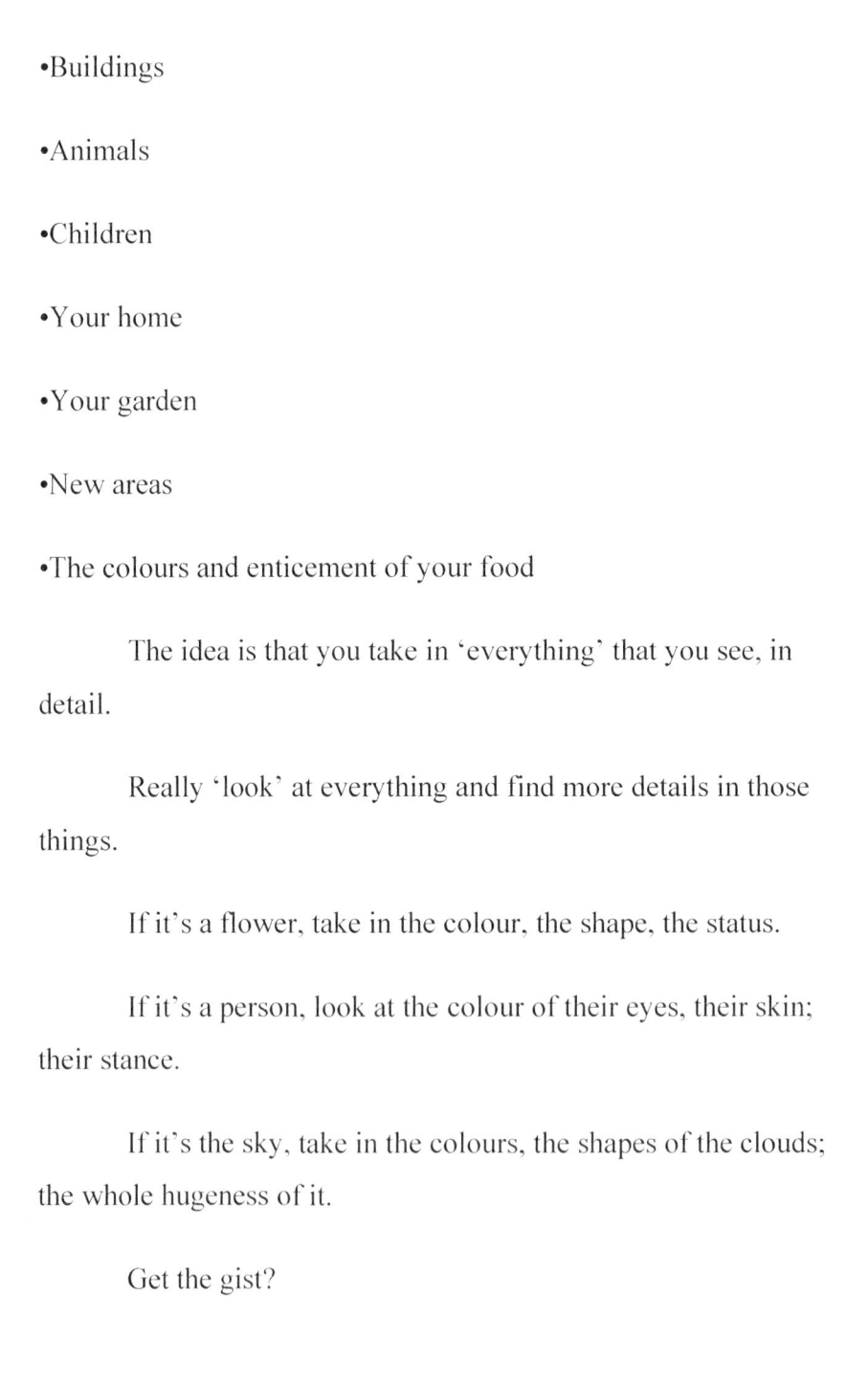

- Animals

- Children

- Your home

- Your garden

- New areas

- The colours and enticement of your food

The idea is that you take in 'everything' that you see, in detail.

Really 'look' at everything and find more details in those things.

If it's a flower, take in the colour, the shape, the status.

If it's a person, look at the colour of their eyes, their skin; their stance.

If it's the sky, take in the colours, the shapes of the clouds; the whole hugeness of it.

Get the gist?

Looking at details surrounding us is soothing and uplifting, so try just doing that today, and I hope you will benefit from it.

Day two – all about taste

I want you to think about everything that you taste today (obviously if you are blessed with the sense of taste)

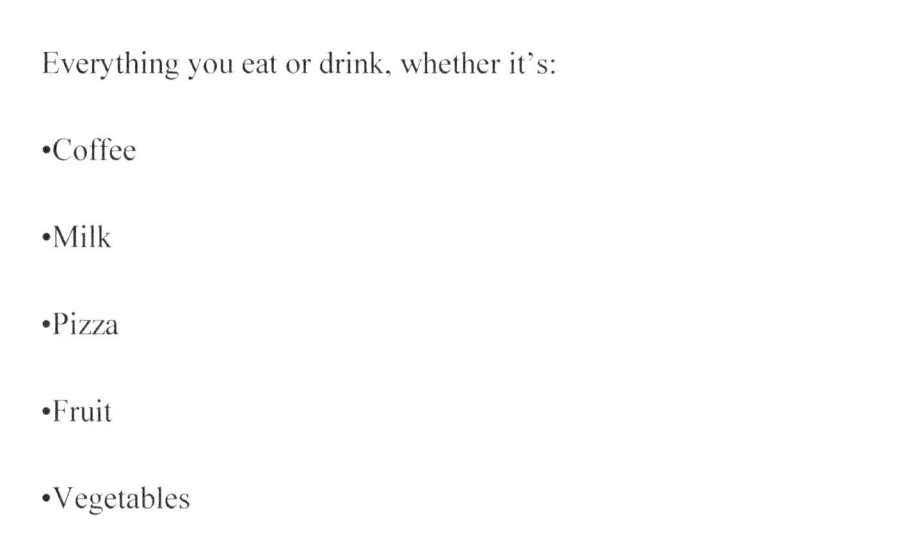

Everything you eat or drink, whether it's:

•Coffee

•Milk

•Pizza

•Fruit

•Vegetables

•Fizzy water

•Orange

•Mints

•Crisps

•Ice cream

The idea is that you take in 'everything' that you taste, in detail (hopefully healthy stuff, despite my mixed list there!)

Really 'taste' everything and enjoy the flavour. Eat or drink 'mindfully'.

This can even be good for eating issues and can be a great comfort for us generally.

If it's a drink, is it warm, cold or hot? Is it strongly flavoured or mild?

If it's food, what texture is it? How does it taste? Is it delicious? If not, why not? Try something else.

Hopefully this is easy for you.

Really tasting our food, chewing it properly, enjoying it – it is all good for our digestion, our feeling of fullness, our comfort within, and it can be soothing and uplifting. So, just try to concentrate on what you taste today and I hope that you will enjoy it as much as I will, because I will do this too.

Day three - all about touch and feeling

I want you to think about everything that you touch today.

It might be:

- Stroking the cat
- Stroking the dog
- Your hair
- Soft dressing gown
- Slippers on your feet
- A cool duvet as you go to sleep
- A tin of food
- A glass
- A mug of hot tea
- An apple
- Computer keyboard
- Toilet cleaner bottle
- Washing the dishes
- Having a bath

Anything at all that you touch – and you will touch many things during a whole day!

However, I want you to go further than what you touch by hand. I want you to think about how your whole body 'feels' whilst:

•Sat in a chair (comfortable, back ache, posture, hard chair…)

•Sat on the sofa (soft, cosy…)

•Sat in the car

•Lying in bed

•At work

•Laying on grass in a park

•The wind blows through your hair

•The sun shines warm on your face

•Walking on hard concrete or spongy grass

So, we are looking at sensations too.

Whilst you are doing anything during the day, are you:

•Cold?

•Warm?

•Hot?

- Sweating?

- Shivering?

Lastly, I would like you to sit comfortably, or lay down preferably, and for a few minutes, just concentrate on how you feel from your toes up to your head, one limb or area at a time. Slowly. Let your back or bum sink into the chair, bed or whatever you are on. Let your arms relax as you take notice of them. Let your head go heavy. Once you have found a relaxed position, just stay there for a few minutes and try to keep focussed on how you feel.

DONE! So if you did all of that, well done! I hope you feel more relaxed!

The more you practise these mindful techniques, the easier it will become for you to reach out to each 'sense'

Day four – all about sound and hearing

I want you to think about everything that you hear today – and this is a huge one!

It might be:

- Alarm clock

- Phone ringing

- People talking in the background

- Conversation with someone

- Cat meowing

- Dog barking

- Children playing

These are fine, but I want you to concentrate on much more than this. I want you to really listen out for ALL noises. If you try hard enough, you will hear things that you would not normally even notice. Things like…

- Birds singing

- Faint train sounds

- Humming of the computer

- A plane going by overhead (wonder where they're going?)

- The 'pitter-patter' of rain on the windows

- Even the lack of sound when it comes to silence

Anything at all that you hear – and you will hear many things during a whole day!

How do these sounds make you feel?

Angry?

Happy?

Agitated?

Soothed?

Our senses are linked with emotions so if we eat something we really like, we may feel comforted, if we hear a slow song we really like, we may feel soothed. If we hear fast, loud music, we may feel energised. If we see a beautiful scene or flower, we may feel uplifted. And so on.

Day five - all about the sense of smell

I want you to think about everything that you smell today. This is one that we do tend to notice more than other senses, as we come across many pungent smells, but we still do not notice everything automatically, so you still have some work to do!

Some obvious ones:

- Toast burning

- Coffee brewing

- Grass after it's been cut

- Fresh smell after it's rained

- Everything you eat

Some will be nice smells, others not so nice, but taking notice of all of them is what is key here.

So concentrate, wherever you go. I want you to really smell everything. Things like…

- The smell inside your car

- The smell of your freshly laundered top as you put it on

- Reach out to smell flowers

- Really inhale the smell of your food

Anything at all that you smell – and you will smell many things during a whole day!

How do these smells make you feel?

Repulsed?

Uplifted?

Soothed?

We can change the way we are feeling because our senses are linked with emotions, so if we wish to feel more relaxed, we can use lavender oils or something that is relaxing for us. If we want to feel uplifted, we can make coffee or wash with fruity shower gels. We may have our own 'comfort' smells and if we are aware of them, then we can use them to our benefit.

Day six – all about using all the senses throughout the day

So, we have come to the last day of my 'Six days to mindfulness and better relaxation – day six is all about using all our five senses consciously.

I want you to think about everything that you smell, taste, feel/touch, see and hear today. This is a hard one in some ways as we often do not have time to take in absolutely everything, but our senses are there all the time if we wish to 'plug in' to them.

•So, really take time to taste anything you eat or drink or chew

•Take in all the smells around you

•Really look around at your surroundings – not to the point of danger if you are driving, but you know what I mean :-)

•Listen out for any sounds, as they are always there

•And finally, be aware of the feeling of everything you come into contact with

I would also like you to be aware of your breathing today, connecting with your own rhythm and your own being.

We can change the way we are feeling because our senses are linked with emotions, so if we wish to feel more relaxed, we can use perfumed oils or something that is relaxing for us, like eating a certain food or going somewhere beautiful in the fresh air. If we want to feel uplifted, we can watch a great film, listen to our favourite music or take a bicycle ride in the sunshine.

Everyone will have their own 'comfort' space or taste or smells and so on, and if we are aware of them, then we can use them to our benefit in everyday life

Have a wonderful day!

How do you feel emotionally?

Uplifted?

Soothed?

Relaxed?

Really connecting with our five senses helps us to enjoy our time and surroundings and allows us to connect with our world more fully.

So, I hope you have enjoyed the six-day journey of my simple 'sense' mindfulness techniques, and that you feel better for practising them. Do keep it up, as practise will instil them in your mind allowing you better enjoyment of your surroundings.

I am using mindfulness a lot more now to keep me stress and depression free each day, by concentrating on what I can smell, hear, taste, see or touch on any given moment. This 'keeps me focussed in the moment' which enables me to keep my mind off negative things.

N is for…

No sale

One very important thing to look out for is impulsive spending or over-spending. It can start off innocent but occasionally it can lead to gambling.

When we feel low, we sometimes get the urge to cheer ourselves up or tell ourselves we are worthy of some retail therapy. This is all well and good if we have copious amounts of money to spend, but if we don't, the outcome can be very depressing indeed, and can also lead to debts we cannot pay off.

It is important to stop this type of spending if we feel, or our loved ones feel, it is, or could get, out of control. Stop it early. Before purchasing something ask yourself "Why am I buying this?" "Why do I want it?" "Do I want it or do I need it?" "Will buying this item make me feel happier?" The latter is just as important as impulse buying can often lead to disappointment and guilt. We get the object home and berate ourselves for spending, checking the bank account, the credit card account, worrying about the bills… It might not be this tight, but basically if you don't have the money, don't go buying unnecessary items, particularly on credit cards. It is always nice to have some money in reserve, no matter how small an amount, just to keep our anxiety at bay.

Personally, if there is something I really WANT rather than need, I have a clear out of things I don't want or need anymore, sell them on *Ebay*, *Gumtree* or through the local newspaper, and then I can make my purchase without guilt. I think it's a lot of fun and certainly more fun than using a credit card!

O is for…

Other inspiring ideas

I was reminded a year or so back by lovely on-line friend, Dody (Doreen Cox, Author of 'Adventures in Mother-sitting') how important it is to keep our eyes and ears open to the positives in our lives – past and present. Because, no matter what adversities life throws at us, if we look hard enough, there are always moments of joy and peace. And that is what I am doing, keeping focused on all the joys amid recent sad times. It works! I cannot recommend it enough!

Every day I hear people moan, see people moan on-line, and most certainly moan myself sometimes. It is very easy to say what we don't like, what we want changed, what's 'not good enough'. Whether it's a trip advisor review, a complaint about the government, a gripe with a family member or a friend has let us down, we just don't seem to stop.

So, a few months ago I decided to say thank you.

Thank you to all doctors, nurses and NHS staff who mended my dad's diseased heart, via a triple heart bypass.

Thank you to all doctors, nurses and NHS staff who whizzed my mum to hospital after her fall, who mended her broken femur, put all her ribs back together, kept her alive, cured her septicaemia, found out her lithium was too high… who basically saved her life.

Thank you to the staff at the dementia home who helped us all to realise my mum's dementia isn't so bad yet and enabled her to get back home.

Thanks to dad for finally agreeing to have mum back and for looking after her – she is now thriving, and everything is much happier than it's been in many years in that house. They get out a lot, mum is on her feet, her mind is better (dementia at bay for now), I see them; all is good.

Thanks to my friend, Anita, for sending me such a kind gift in the post.

Thanks to all my friends (on-line and in person) who lend me an ear if I need it and help me along in life.

Thanks to my boyfriend for being with me throughout the 3-month ordeal with my mum.

I am thankful to have a home and my pets.

I am thankful that I can eat and drink every day.

I am thankful that I have relative freedom in my life.

I am thankful that I had my Auntie Ciss in my life, albeit not now.

I am thankful I have a car.

I am thankful for my health (OK I have some issues, but… I am still alive)

I also feel thankful to live in the UK.

I know there are a lot of things we can moan about, when it comes to politics, misspending, benefits etc BUT all in ALL it's a pretty safe country, we have varied weather without too much devastation, we have a great NHS really (even if they have let me down sometimes), people are looked after via a benefit system (which, let's face it, could never work like clockwork) Yes, there's poverty, but most countries have poverty. We have lots of charities helping those that the government cannot, like the one I work at; helping the homeless. The only shame is how many of us are so materialistic (guilty here).

I almost want to say what I don't like, but sometimes we just have to choose to be thankful, rather than complain – we have the choice whether we look for positives or negatives, just as we can choose to fight or give up.

What are you thankful for today?

A spring clean and clear out – de-clutter your house, wardrobes and minds and maybe even help a charity in the process!

More ideas that can be good for the mind, body and soul…

So, I have talked about many inspiring ways to help one's mental health; things everyone could benefit from such as looking after pets, gardening or keeping indoor or outdoor potted plants. And I have talked about having days out where you can learn new things, take in history, arts or just some fresh air.

And now I am promoting a good old spring clean and clear out!

OK we all know about spring cleaning and how lovely it is when your house is all sparkly, furniture moved to different places and smelling fresh, but a clear out at the same time is simply marvellous.

Usually I have a clear out in order to do boot sales and give some to charity, but after twenty-two years of boot sales since I was eighteen, I had enough of them – even the lazy bones ones – as it was a lot of hard work for very little at times.

I have actually been clearing out all year, but having swapped my summer clothes for winter jumpers (I always keep the out of season clothes in suitcases under my bed) I found more clothes I no longer want. So, I advertised them on-line and earnt a few more pounds, which I need right now. I have sold a whole lot more and the other bric-a-brac and books I am taking to a charity shop (I tend to rotate the charity shops I give to in order to give to a different one each time).

So, my house gets tidier and tidier, and the pile of stuff to sell gets smaller leaving me more room for storage and I get my little buzz from helping a charity; t makes me feel good!

P is for…

Pets and animals

There are many natural things we can do to improve our mental health; exercise, hobbies, socialising, relaxation techniques or learning new coping skills are some examples. Another very helpful experience can be looking after or seeing animals (if you like animals that is).

There are schemes like 'animal assisted therapy' where a dog, or other animal, is present to calm or enliven patients or clients. But, aside from the professional links, animals can be like 'therapy' for many people – dogs, hamsters, horses, all sorts.

I personally love all animals, but cats are my chosen favourite. You don't have to own them either, you can foster! Fostering cats is such a wonderful thing to do as there are far too many cats and kittens out there needing homes. As many as possible are taken in by rescue charities and cared for in house or in external catteries. By fostering, you are housing a cat and allowing the charity to house one more from whatever adversity it is going through. The same goes for many other types of pet too.

I fostered Titus nearly two years ago and felt he was the one for me so I couldn't let him go and adopted him. One of the best decisions I have ever made. I recently adopted Millie, my kitten, too, and she is a real sweetie.

I really wanted Titus to be a therapy cat, but he is not of the right nature as he has mood swings. But he is, kind of, a therapy cat to my mum and dad when I take him round there. I get dinner, they get my cat and I for the night. They actually ask me to bring him. Dad strokes him, teases him and plays with him (usually getting a scratch or two!) and Mum follows him around, cooing over him and strokes him; albeit timidly at times. It struck me that Titus is a kind of therapy cat in those situations. My cats are definitely therapy for me and a whole lot of fun with their cheeky ways and imaginative ways of communicating their needs. They fill my life with joy. But, when I take Titus to my mum and dads, he fills their house with joy as well. No problems; just calm, fun and enjoyment.

Pets are great for mental health and wellbeing!

You and your pet (s) get satisfaction from the unspoken love you share, you feel responsible for the animal and they can be great fun! They do not have to be hard work (I have no children and live alone so I can afford the time), but you should be willing to care for them, to the best of your abilities for their entire lives, if you can, as it's not fair to take on animals just because they are cute kittens or puppies just to get bored of them in a year or two. But if you can then they can be soothing, fun and great company.

Oh by the way, as told in the 'Secret Life of Cats' TV show… Cat owners are a third less likely to suffer from heart disease because the act of stroking a cat creates the stress busting enzyme called 'renin' which slows our heart rate down and reduces our blood pressure.

MINDFULNESS… Watching a cat rolling on the floor, listening to their purring, stroking their soft fur is wonderful; they are relaxing to watch, relaxing to hear and relaxing to touch and that's three of our five senses being stimulated. Using the senses is one very simple stress coping skill – if we can stimulate our senses, in a mindful way, we take our mind off worries, problems and unwanted thoughts.

A cat is also a companion and they don't ask for much apart from comfort and food and a bit of a fuss.

Of course not ALL cats are calm, so don't quote me on that, some can be vicious or uninterested, but I speak of the majority.

I have tropical fish too, and would have a dog if I had a garden. I had to say goodbye to my hamster recently which was sad… But, I like to think that I have enhanced their lives as much as they have mine.

I speak of cats, but there are many animals that can be looked after as pets, and if having a pet is not possible then maybe seeing them in the wild or in animal centres could be soothing and fun. I adored my little hamster, Molly, who passed earlier this year. From little to large, there's a pet for everyone who likes animals.

Q is for…

Questions

I write this to encourage people with depressed or anxious moods to talk to those around them, and vice versa, if it is apt to. Find out how your behaviours affect your loved ones and how they feel about you. Also, suggest they ask questions so that you can explain to them how it feels for you as an individual, and how they might be able to help you. Having a better understanding of each other will lead to better relationships.

Talking really does help.

R is for…

Relax

We can all keep busy to keep our minds off all sorts of problems in our lives BUT always remember it's also very beneficial to just stop, stay still, and let our minds wander on their own for a while. Some of my best ideas have come to me when essentially 'doing nothing' – some of my best writing ideas, answers to questions and I have even solved some of those underlying problems that had been bugging me sub consciously.

Try 'doing nothing' today – just 20/30 minutes. If nothing else, it will most likely refresh your mind ready for the day.

Relaxing is also time when you invest in your hobbies (see separate chapter for hobbies), when you are eating (aiding digestion) and sleeping. Take time out to relax before sleeping and you may well sleep better.

S is for…

Sing! Singing and music are a therapy of their own

Singing, a bit like shouting, is a way of letting yourself go. The difference, of course, is that it's far more positive than shouting, which just fuels anger and adrenalin production. Singing along to your favourite songs in the car, at home, whilst cooking, is relaxing.

Whether it's *Gotan Project* or *Deep Forest*, *Rhianna* or *Psy*, dance, hip hop, pop, rock, ballad's, bring it on. I own music for every mood, I know music for memories, good, bad and sad, and I know music works for others as therapy as I have tried it out many times. So turn off the TV and play some music – relax, dance or remember.

T is for…

Therapies and counselling

So, what exactly is counselling?

"Counselling is not advising, gossiping or argument about anything. That's chatting. Counselling is unbiased support"

Counselling occurs when a person (client) seeks the help of another (counsellor) and engages in private conversations with them in order to resolve issues in their life. A therapeutic relationship is key where the client feels at ease to share their problems with the counsellor and the counsellor listens, seeks to understand the problems from the client's point of view (empathy) and gives them the space to explore their feelings, thoughts and behaviours. Important within this relationship is that the client is active and ready to engage with the counsellor in sessions. If they are not, then counselling does not occur. It is not about having a 'chat', it is about exploring issues, looking at thought processes, and a desire to change negative patterns.

I have had counselling on numerous occasions, as a client, and have mainly been open and honest about myself, my issues and negative personality traits as I see them. However, with one counsellor, I was not totally honest and held back information about my behaviours so as to protect myself. This stopped a counselling relationship to fully occur and I could not be helped with some of my issues – if the counsellor isn't told, they cannot help.

I feel that if a person really wants to change their negative thoughts, feelings and actions regarding an issue in their life, that a talking therapy such as counselling, is one of the best opportunities the person will have. This relies on the therapeutic relationship forming, and a feeling of trust and confidentiality being experienced by the client. Counselling can help with many issues, including finding a path to a life worth living for the client.

Some clients need little more than someone to talk to; to bounce their ideas off, to be listened to intently, to be understood and accepted for who they are. Merely talking and having their words said back to them via paraphrasing, could be enough, as the client resolves their own issues. This could lead to short term counselling requirements.

Other clients need a lot more. They may take much longer to soak up their realities. They may be in denial; thus requiring repetition in order to break through their barriers, to see the errors in their thinking. They may need help to explore what are 'actually' the issues in their lives. For example, if depressed, a person may experience 'catastrophizing' where they view everything that happens in their lives as a problem. They cannot 'see the wood for the trees' and simply do not have the calmness or insight to work out which are real problems and which are just in their mind, a problem that isn't actually a problem at all. This is irrational thinking and the counsellor may need to challenge the client many times in order for the client to see their errors in their thinking; the reality of the situation.

People naturally judge others, and because of this, sometimes stigma or bullying can occur, usually borne from ignorance. Therefore, many people fear talking to others' in case they think they are bad or wrong. People we know well are often biased; either wanting to protect us, or tell us we are wrong, and it's commonplace to be judged. We may go to these people for advice, but it is much more comfortable and helpful if we can talk to someone without bias. If the counsellor is patient, calm, empathic, a good listener, and is not shocked by what the client tells them, the client is more likely to open up further and explore their thoughts, feelings, and actions with honesty and feel more self-worth which can aid social inclusion.

A counsellor will treat each client as an individual, with individual needs, thoughts, feelings and behaviours and the therapeutic relationship will be based on allowing and helping the client to make their own decisions and find their own answers. The counsellor will aid them in doing this via challenging questions, verifying information and much more. A trained counsellor, however, may possess knowledge of coping skills, which could be explained to the client, if suitable and relevant to the client's needs.

In any case, it is not the role of the counsellor to advise the client what to do, or to share their own experiences or views.

I find that by following the practise of counselling, by studying and learning, and by self-reflection, I enter each of my counselling sessions at ease -- comfortable, and with a determination to help my clients, and this helps me to be a good counsellor. My clients are open and honest with me, they are as committed as am I, they trust me, they are not afraid to show or share their emotions and deepest thoughts, and they are willing and open for the challenges I may set them with their agreement. They understand what counselling means to them fairly quickly, and as we meet more and more, and they overcome some of their issues, they become even more determined to help themselves within sessions, outside of session time, and after our relationship and meetings end.

Having been through lots of adversities in my forty-two years, and having seen family members and friends going through as many, I am very resilient, which I feel is important as a counsellor. I remain calm and not shocked by what my clients tell me. I do not judge my clients. And this helps the client feel at ease. If they can trust me in telling me of their adversities and stories (testing the water with me), and the result of my interaction is calm, helpful and insightful, then they open up more and give me more of their truths. These are things you should look for when seeking a counsellor, and during sessions.

Types of counselling and talking therapies

There are various treatments on offer – I will talk about the ones I have experienced:

Cognitive behavioural therapy (CBT) – I have spoken about CBT in depth, in chapter C for CBT, but just to re-iterate… When we are depressed, we can view the world, ourselves and the future negatively, which keeps us depressed. The pattern of negativity has to be broken. CBT works on core beliefs that we have and our thoughts affect our behaviour and actions. If we say to ourselves 'I can't ride a bike' then we won't even try, and then we will be hard on ourselves for not trying, consider ourselves a failure, and so on. And even if we try to ride a bike, at the first fall or mistake, we will say that it just proves we cannot do it, and we cement the idea in our brain.

However, if we change the thought to 'I will be able to ride a bike' then we will at least try and go from there. If we fall or make a mistake, we will be able to look past it and try again.

CBT focuses on identifying dysfunctional thinking and change it so that our behavioural patterns will change. Then we can begin to change the symptoms that keep us depressed – stop the vicious circle as it were. Often, the best effects will come after therapy has finished, as it sinks in, over time, and becomes a new way of thinking and behaving.

Psychotherapy – this individual therapy focuses on the relationships the person with depression has with other people. It can also delve into childhood experiences to find answers as to the formation of depression and relationship issues or other negative problems. I have found the talking and unearthing of the past useful, but also detrimental if we unearthed things and didn't continue the therapy long enough to deal with those things or understand them. This is why I wrote my memoir in the end. Psychotherapy can be intense, and is usually not a short term therapy, so commitment and the ability to stick with it, financially and physically, is important in my opinion.

Humanistic/person centred counselling – this one to one therapy is based on talking with a person trained to listen with empathy and acceptance. I had around one year of person-centred counselling, and found it very useful as he was supportive and I had someone to talk to who didn't judge me. He was empathic, gave me his full attention and was all the things a counsellor should be, like being unbiased. That was so important for me, as everyone else in my personal life was biased and I could not speak to them about my issues. For one, they wouldn't understand (and yes I did try to explain about myself to them, a little) and two, I was ashamed of myself. The way it works is to talk about your feelings and actions in order to find out your own solutions to things. The counsellor does not give you the answers, but listens and guides the conversations, challenging you if required. It is all about helping the client feel better; about them as an individual.

As I counsellor, I am trained to be integrative, which means I use all three of the above theories and I have to say, most of the time more than one theory is useful for each client.

There are also many other talking therapies to choose from.

When thinking about whether to have talking therapy or not, and wondering if it might be too much to handle, think about this…

To risk or not to risk – both are just as risky actually! 'Balancing Risks' in your life.

During a counselling session with a client, he was saying that he wants to change his life yet fears making changes and taking risks in case of negative outcomes. He says that it is safer to stay the same. He can stay in his comfort zone if he doesn't take risks or make changes even though he knows it is not a comfort to stay the same at all. He feels he doesn't want to push himself.

I explained the reverse psychology of risk taking... By NOT doing something/taking a risk, we might actually be taking an equal risk. For example, one of his dilemmas was:

"If I look for other relationships, the outcome might be that they leave me, or it doesn't work out well, or they might pass away and make me feel sad and lonely (negative automatic thoughts about possible outcomes)

BUT, I offered him another way to look at it, based on things he had already confirmed himself during our sessions:

"If I don't look for other relationships, I might be lonely, have low self-esteem, miss out on wonderful shared times and I will have no-one to give my support to" (just as negative as above)

The thing is if we do nothing, we just stay the same and do not have the opportunity to enjoy the positives, which in this example are: being in social company, having better confidence, enjoying great times and having people to care about.

We might avoid risks by staying in, in case we get run over, but it might be just as likely (which is actually very unlikely) to harm ourselves in the home. It is a risk to DO and a risk to NOT DO.

Therefore, the risks can be just as negative, just in different ways, but NOT DOING ANYTHING is as conscious a decision as DOING SOMETHING.

So, before you decide to avoid change or avoid taking a risk, maybe weighing it up in this way can help you to re-evaluate whether to act or not act upon it. I say this not just for the question of whether to take up talking therapy or not, but it can be used in many aspects of the decisions we make in life.

I'm going to call this evaluation 'Balancing Risks'.

Would it be a risk not to have talking therapy or would it be a risk to have a talking therapy? Which outcome would be more beneficial?

U is for…

Understanding and Empathy

By 'understanding', I mean our understanding of how we are with others' and how our behaviours might affect them, so that we can become more self-aware. And by empathy, I mean trying to gain an understanding how someone else feels, so that we can understand their reactions better. Empathy is like a comfort blanket we can offer someone without the emotion of sympathy, which is where we might say how sorry we are or sad we are that someone feels a certain way. Empathy is far more powerful than sympathy when it comes to helping others' so next time someone gets angry, sad or upset, try to understand why they might feel those things. We are ALL individuals, and cannot put our own ethics and thoughts onto others. Everyone feels and thinks their own way, and unless we try to empathise with them, we can only judge them based on ourselves and how we would react or deal with things that happen to us.

So, if you lost your job and coped well, it doesn't mean that someone else will. You might be in £1000 debt and feel like it's a major trauma, and someone else wouldn't care if they were in debt £1000. Each person will have their own feelings and thoughts, background and circumstances surrounding a traumatic, sad, upsetting event, and their reactions will be individual too. By understanding and empathising with others' we can learn so much about ourselves as self-awareness too!

V is for…

Vitamins and minerals

Getting the right vitamins and minerals is important. There are even some foodstuffs, containing vitamins and minerals that help with mental health issues. I am no expert on this subject, so all I will do here is share what I do. I cannot recommend, but it works for me. You need to find out about your best nutrition requirements and seek your GP's help if required.

Here's one of my favourite milkshake recipes – all it consists of is one banana, some semi-skimmed milk (or soya, but I cannot have it with because I take Thyroxine and soya milk stops the thyroxine working properly) and 2 pieces of dark 70% dark chocolate, which needs to be at least room temperature or it will not blend well. Blend the whole lot together and give yourself a few minutes to yourself to enjoy the frothy delight. YUM!

And, the brilliant thing is that it is great for serotonin production (natural anti-depressant basically) – bananas and chocolate are both 'feel good' foods and bananas are full of potassium, selenium and B vitamins, as well as countless other nutrients. Calcium in the milk… Need I say more… Go on, treat yourself!

I also love making fruit smoothies. They are absolutely delicious and packed with goodness. I use a banana as a base 'superfood' Then I might add melon, strawberries, blueberries (marvellous anti-oxidant) or raspberries.

With my smoothie, I take Lactobacillus Acidophilus (at the moment a combined 'blend' bead called 'Probiotic Acidophilus') which is great for my IBS (Irritable Bowel Syndrome). I have been taking it for years now and when I had some tummy issues I realised that I had stopped taking it for about six weeks so promptly went out and bought some more. I do have probiotic yoghurt but not every day so it clearly wasn't enough to keep my gut in good order and full of healthy bacteria. However, I have just been bought a yoghurt maker so I am enjoying far more probiotic yoghurt now, and it's all good stuff when made at home.

I also take a Co-Enzyme Q10 to try to aid the production of energy from my food (trying to compensate for the lack of energy I have due to my 'Hypothyroidism' (under active thyroid) and a milk thistle to cleanse my liver due to all the alcohol I used to drink. Then throughout the day I might take an anti-oxidant such as Selenium with A, C and E and I take zinc and Echinacea to fend off colds and infection.

I have my smoothie after one cup of tea and a fresh coffee. Oh, and if I am in a really good mood or want to get into a good mood, I put some music on and have a little dance and sing-a-long – it does work, give it a go sometime! Very energising for mind, body and soul.

I eat lots of lettuce too, which contains sleep-inducing qualities. It contains an opium-related chemical, and thus possesses mild sedative properties. Lettuce also contains *hyoscyamine* which is an anti-cramping agent that also helps promote relaxed muscles, plus calcium and potassium, both stress fighting nutrients.

It is a fantastic addition to an evening meal, not only does it aid restful sleep but it is fresh, nutritious and very low in calories.

I use Bach's flower remedies, for calming and for 'get up and go' and I love them. Always read the label of course.

There are so many vitamins and foodstuffs that can help mental health, I would need to write a whole book about them, so I will leave these with you and can advise that there are some very good articles on-line and books about foods for good mental health, anti-stress, depression and much more. I would highly recommend taking a look.

W is for…

Writing Therapy (Expressive and Creative)

I have enjoyed writing short stories since I was very young. When I read some of them now, I wonder where my ideas came from; a very young child writing about a scary place in the woods…

I now know that my stories probably came from fear and stress, and at the age of thirteen I began writing a diary. I kept my diaries under lock and key, save anyone EVER reading them, as they were secret, spilling my inner thoughts, feelings and behaviours at times. I could 'talk' to my diary about family life, where I'd been, what I'd done, what clothes I'd worn, and most of all if any adversities came my way – like my mum causing issues, boyfriends taking advantage, my brothers' behaviours', rape, self-harm, eating disorder and so on – they were all written down, which kind of 'saved' me at the time.

I found that by writing what was happening in my life, it was like talking to a friend – an unbiased friend who would never say a word against me. Like a good counsellor. Therefore, I felt less lonely in my family life, I got to express myself, and leave my troubles behind in writing on the paper. I felt relief from my troubles and the next day I could start afresh.

I have written ever since, via diary, journal, blogging, letters sent and unsent and more.

I then wrote a couple of memoirs, and in doing so, I had to write and re-write various events. Some were traumatic, and brought about very strong emotions. Some were forgotten about; one in particular because of the trauma it caused. That was dissociation. But, what I found was, the more I wrote and re-wrote and edited, the less the issues bothered me.

I also began to look at the benefits of writing, for me. I found many:

1. The way to talk to someone without worrying about what others' think.

2. The way to explore how I feel and think and, ultimately, behave – gaining insight and revelations on how I can change things.

3. I can look at my writing the next day, week, month or years later, and see how far I have come – how much happier I am or how much I have achieved.

4. It can help me to see things from other people's points of view – a more rounded opinion.

5. It built my self-esteem.

6. Writing has been self-therapy for me – very cathartic

7. I have been able to look back and remember things I would never have usually recalled, good and bad – a bit like taking photos and finding them again.

8. I wrote unsent letters to people passed and alive, and told them everything I wanted to get off my chest, positive and negative, any apologies and anything I wanted to tell them or even ask them. The main point was that I wasn't going to send them, so I disclosed totally.

9. Writing unsent letters helped me to see who I was through my writing; to find myself and what is important to me.

10. Writing letters was like having a chat with them, but disclosing much more than I would have had we really been having a chat.

My Client case study

My client, BS, has had trouble describing his emotions to me. More than that, he was not sure what they were, as he was not in touch with them. But this has changed…

By session sixteen, it became apparent that talking therapies (person-centred counselling, psychodynamic therapy and CBT) could be boosted with the use of writing therapy. I had already tapped into his emotions by looking at some of his art work (drawings) as he is a keen artist. I asked him to bring in some of his work, and he did so the very next week, keen to share his drawings with me. They were brilliant and as a result, he was able to describe some emotions around drawing them and looking at them currently.

BS had lost sight of who he was, personality wise, and was afraid of change. CBT sheets showed up BS's catastrophizing traits, and helped him to notice his irrational thinking. I introduced writing therapy and gave BS a sheet to take home about how to write and why it helps.

"Overall, writing is a challenge for you, but when a challenge is overcome and writing done, you will have achieved, you have taken control and fought negatives that tell you that you cannot do it. It builds self-esteem and you will win a 'low risk' challenge"

BS mentioned how an art tutor once said not to think too much about what to draw, but just to doodle and see what happens and I said that this is very similar to that and that I chose writing over art because art is already a hobby for him and a comfort and writing is not, so it's more of a challenge.

He found it hard writing stories at School, so I said that the best results come from those who initially find writing hard and write in a muddled way like him.

BS wrote about past traumas and found it very helpful to put closure on the trauma, to understand it from his, and the other person's point of view, and he has found insight about his feelings as they flowed onto paper. It shocked him to re-read these emotions and also realise that positives come from negatives, he has made huge progress and can stop himself from running away from issues by quick realisation that he is doing it. He feels more adult and more equal.

So, going back to my personal experience, were all the benefits I found from writing found overall in studies? YES!

Expressive Writing is a form of writing therapy developed primarily by James W. Pennebaker in the late 1980s. Over three hundred studies have been carried out on Expressive Writing Therapy, especially for those who have experienced trauma. A major result is that the people end up going to the doctor less afterwards, they work better, sleep better and have better relationships.

     Arthritis, Irritable bowel symptoms, reduced stress and resting blood pressure are proven to be some of the many problems aided by expressive writing.

I often found that after writing, especially if it was about a trauma or upsetting event, I felt worse (sad or angry) but after it all sank in and

I reflected, I felt more relieved and had a better understanding of myself and other people. It helped me to come out of denial too.

If something really bothered me, I might ruminate and go over it. In writing my memoirs I had to write and re-write everything and every time I did, my feelings and reactions to the experiences and traumas become less and less affecting. Writing about my experiences over and over for my memoirs really numbed me to most of my traumas, and this can occur with expressive writing therapy too.

Of course, when I re-worked sections for my memoir, I had an audience (my readers) in mind, but the beauty of expressive writing therapy actually comes from 'disclosure' where we write something JUST for our own eyes; so we don't have to think about what other people think about us, their biases, how they will react, or how we might affect them. If you are to gain the best benefits, you will write just for YOURSELF.

As I mentioned in my list above, I wrote unsent letters to everyone important in my life: friends, family even therapists (alive or passed away), to tell them how I really felt about certain things. I would write a separate letter every day and I told them everything I wanted to say in an unbiased, 'get it all out' style with an almost formal approach to it, yet full of my emotions, thoughts and feelings. Everything laid out on the paper or computer screen in the written word. Permanent, yet unsent. The person will never see the letter, yet it's a great release to have written it.

But these are things I could never say directly to them. Weeks or months later, I repeated the exercise to see if I feel better about them. Since I felt so negatively about most people, I thought it would be a good way to analyse whether I have beaten my negativity and I most often had.

Another form of writing I find helpful are lists; it can be a way to really 'see' what is going on, so I can evaluate what I am thinking in a more balanced way. I write down what has been stressing me (negative) and what is positive in my life. Making lists has really helped me to concentrate on the positives, but also understand the negatives, and why some things are 'getting on top of me' especially because I did not deal with 'changes in life' or 'boredom' well.

Near the end of a year, I write down all the things I have achieved in the past year, against a list I made at the beginning of that year of 'targets to achieve'. I must say it pleases me to take time out to reflect, as it is so easy to let time pass and feel that you are getting nowhere. I then write a new list of what I want to happen in the following year – a goal to go for. It keeps me focussed.

And it is when I look at all that I HAVE done (rather than the negatives of what I have NOT done/what I have failed at, and all the adversities of the past year, that I can see just how motivated I can be, just how much I can achieve and how much joy I have had. I decided 'I will stop using the word 'CAN'T' because I most likely CAN!' I was then able to take on more responsibility too!

If you are interested in learning more about expressive writing therapy, I highly recommend this book 'Expressive Writing Words that Heal by James W Pennebaker PHD and John F Evans EDD' Pennebaker'.

Years ago when I took up a few weeks of career counselling, during another of my 'I don't know what to do in life' procrastinations, I learnt some useful tricks to feed my self-esteem and help me with decisions around my work.

    I was advised to write some lists about myself and my skills – an idea which I then manipulated to suit my needs.

    First of all, I wrote down all major events and things I'd done throughout my life. This really showed up just how many experiences I'd had and events that had occurred during my life to date. It was great to remember past holidays, travel, births, jobs, family events and achievements, such as parachute jumps, diving and learning to swim better. I could see I'd had fun, and had had courage to take up challenges.

It was also helpful to see how adversities had affected me, like the death of a family member or personal ill health, and realising how I had managed to get over those adversities boosted my strength and confidence to take on all that was thrown at me, from then on, in a positive way.

I then wrote down all my skills in life – work or otherwise. This incorporated everything from travelling alone and learning languages to PC skills and customer service experience. That list, surprisingly, got very long. And as it did, my self-esteem grew.

Next was 'What I like doing'. So this was not just about what I CAN do, but what I actually like to do. This helped me to recognise skills that could be utilised in a job or in hobbies, which would be an enjoyable job for me – what I really like doing.

Next came the list 'What I dislike doing'. Now this may seem a little negative, but it highlighted things that got me down and shed some light on tasks that I could delegate, and if this was not possible, to change my attitude towards the task. Changing a negative to a positive is so rewarding and I was able to find ways to make some niggling jobs a little more pleasant. A simple example would be 'I find washing up boring'. So, I decided to change the time of day I washed the dishes – to the morning instead of evening – and put on my favourite music while I washed up. It then became an enjoyable thing to do with my first cup of tea of the day. It also stopped me from wallowing in bed, delaying getting started for the day ahead and making myself late (although that is another story!).

Of course, not everyone is in the position to change jobs, seek out their dream job, or make big changes in their lives BUT the whole exercise of writing down skills and likes/dislikes has helped me in my daily life. It has also helped me to form hobbies and interests outside of work and to see my skills laid out really boosted my confidence. Too many of us are negative about our abilities, but these lists can really highlight just how many we have. I am not a mother, but just thinking about what I would write if I were, well, the list would be endless! Raising a baby is the ultimate in responsibility.

When doing this exercise for the first time, in my twenties, my new found confidence pushed me to go for a management role which was much more responsibility than I had been used to. I got the job and was given a substantial pay rise within six months which I asked for. Those lists made me assertive and gave me a real sense of just how many skills I had to give an employer.

So all this brings me onto the question of 'Should we aim high or not when we have a lack of self-esteem, or mental illness, or anytime our confidence is lacking?

Above I have talked about how writing these lists helped me to recognise my strengths and weaknesses, likes and dislikes, and how they helped me to aim higher in my work at the time, which worked out good. But what I didn't say is that sometimes my depression got in the way.

What happened for me was that I woke every day in my management role and wished I didn't have the responsibility. I dreaded work and that my staff relied on me to fill them with enthusiasm when I had none of my own to share. I truly didn't want to be alive most days and lost all love for myself. Other events were factors in this kind of breakdown, and I left that job – that job that was going so well, paying well and had seen me living alone in a 3 bed house and affording it for once. I had, I decided, taken on too much. But was it just that? Would I have left any job and run home to mum and dad even if it didn't have such responsibility, given my depression, or was it the responsibility that tipped me over the edge? It's hard to say.

What I do know is that I have been driven to get over adversities and ill health, essentially, by my dreams and aspirations, and have achieved a lot and made great progress, by following them. So my failures are far outweighed by the highs and achievements I have experienced. I cannot imagine what would happen if I stopped dreaming and aiming high. And these dreams do not need to be grand or out of reach. When I was mentally tortured by negative symptoms, for example, my dream was simple "I want to have a life worth living' – that was it. And because I didn't have a life worth living at the time, and half the time wanted out of my life, this really was a big dream. But by repeating it to myself, writing it down and aspiring to it every day, progress was made towards it, and now I can say that "I do have a life worth living".

Yes, depression still crept in over the years, shocking me, lashing my brain and wellbeing, bringing me back to feeling hopeless and worthless again, but, essentially, I know that when it passes, (and it passes more quickly each time) I will still have a life worth living.

So, I have talked about Expressive writing therapy, writing letters, lists and more. So I would like to talk about another type of writing, 'Creative Writing', which can be written for any audience. It can be shared, unlike expressive writing therapy. It could result in a blog post, an article, a book, poetry, and more. Much research has been done into the benefits of Art Therapies, including painting, drawing, photography, creative writing and a whole range of arts like pottery, and the benefits include social gains because the art can be shared.

It might be that you share some of your work on-line with others, which increases social interactions. But, even more so, if you attend an art class or group, you not only get feedback on your work, and can gain knowledge for others, the social aspects of communicating in groups, making friends, getting out of the house, and being inspired, can be great for mental health. I talk from my own experience of sharing my writing on-line (blogs), writing articles, books, and attending writing courses at college and writing retreats away from home. I have increased my confidence and self-worth from all of these activities.

Participating in a group activity is a very rewarding, confidence building and sociable way to recover from mental health issues. It helps me to realise why going to college for writing courses and going on writing retreats helped my self-esteem – to share my writing, which is, essentially my art.

One in particular was four week writing course at college and I loved it: creative writing. I would read my work out and get feedback, whilst learning new skills. We concentrated on writing short stories, and how to get them published. This led me to writing a few more short stories; another route to self-expression.

Here's one of my journals about starting my first creative writing college course five years ago, when I was suffering with depression and anxiety a lot. Since then, I have been doing college courses every year and I love it. I am sharing it because even if writing is not your thing, there may be other courses you could do part-time at college. You could find just as many positives doing other courses as

I did doing my writing courses or even by volunteering for a charity or joining an interest group. I hope this journal inspires you…

I took a deep breath, plastered my signature smile on my face and checked my posture before entering through the classroom door, to greet my new teacher and fellow students. (There were only six of us.)

That bit was fine, and I quickly took a seat, hellos and apologies out of the way, then came the bit I dreaded; the formal introductions.

"Welcome to the 'writing your life' class. First of all, let's get to grips with who you are and why you are here, so that we can all make the most of the four sessions over the next four weeks. Please state your name, why you are in the class and anything you would particularly like to focus on – who would like to go first?"

Since I have spent my life attention seeking, it may seem a little strange that I still had issues when all eyes and ears were focussed on me, but I've always been the same – as she spoke I started shaking, my temperature rose, my breath became irregular, yet I knew I wanted to get it over and done with so I quickly volunteered.

I introduced myself and continued "…and I want to write my life story to help me understand my depression. I started to write my childhood two years ago, in 2006, and managed twenty-three thousand words, but I got to an upsetting scene and couldn't write anymore. I have collected memorabilia and communications as well as writing diaries and journals since I was fourteen years old, and now I would like to make some sense of my life through them."

The other women listened intently, keeping eye contact with me as I spoke a little shakily, and they smiled as I finished. Then it was their turn to speak, one by one.

I realised I was drifting off with my thoughts again instead of concentrating. I found it hard to focus. One woman was writing to get over her tormented childhood, two women who wanted to gain some writing skills as a personal hobby, and finally a woman who wanted to document her interesting childhood growing up in a caravan while their house was being built and the way outsiders perceived them as a family at that time.

We did a writing exercise, to describe our childhood home, read out what we'd written and finished up with a homework assignment. I love homework so I was most happy about this. The two and half hour session complete, I left the room feeling uplifted, optimistic and excited – I could do this, I told myself, which was quite a contrast to the person who had walked into the room. They liked my essay describing my childhood home and said that it sounded like there were 'family issues' hidden in my portrayal of how my home looked and felt.

Two weeks later, and the people at my writing class seemed to like what I transcribed from memory, even though it is serious subject matter. I wrote my memory as a little six-year-old girl, in the car with my dad going home after a visit to my mum in the psychiatric hospital. They thought it poignant, that it posed questions and made them want to read more and the tutor agreed, particularly praising my piece describing my family home as well. I felt shivers of satisfaction through my body as they spoke about me so encouragingly. I liked the class – it got me out of the house, I concentrated on my writing and I liked meeting and mixing with people again. I felt like part of society once more. I had not been out to work for a long time by then as I had been working from home on my websites, and had hardly any friends left, so my social life consisted mainly of just my boyfriend and my mum and dad. I felt a bit embarrassed writing about myself. I mean, who was I? No celebrity. Who wanted to read about me? I wasn't special. But, everyone in the class was writing their memoirs and they all had a story to tell. Who doesn't? We have all lived and learnt so much, we all have stories inside our minds. All the while, I beavered away at home, delving, researching and writing my life and I began to feel confident in my writing skills.

I wrote the memoir called 'My Alien Self; My Journey Back to Me' followed by a sequel, simply called '39' because I wrote it at that age. Reviews flooded in, as did comments from people telling me how they felt less alone with their problems after reading about my issues, how many similarities they had to myself and my story, or even just how they have learnt more about stigma and how to avoid it. Big things can be achieved if you go for it!

There's so much more to 'Creative Art Therapy' (drawing, painting, crafts, drama and more), which can be helpful for trauma, PTSD, Dementia and Alzheimer's, relationship issues, self-esteem, depression, anxiety and more. It appears to be a very powerful therapy, and I know that, in self-help, the writing side of art therapy has helped me tremendously.

X is for…

X marks the signs

This follows on from finding out about yourself. It's about recognising the signs for your symptoms, if you can. One of my internal processes begins with me getting stressed, then that stress becomes out of proportion as I become over anxious about even small things. But lots of small things build the stress, like bricks. To the outside world people might think that I am over-reacting to something small, but for me it's not the small thing that has just occurred, it is just the LAST thing I can handle after the last brick topples me. After that I get a day of feeling more energetic and happy, dancing and feeling positive. Then I might come down with the crash of a depressive stage, but it will only last for a day or so. I know it well enough now that even if I feel like my life is terrible and I have no future worth having, I do know also that it will not last long and 'tomorrow is another day'. Things will definitely get better. I have reminders around the house, or chat to people who can remind me to try to ensure I don't forget. However, it's easy to ignore if I feel too down.

So, that is a typical routine for me. How about you? Could you write a journal so that you can analyse your routines? Could you mark on the calendar good days, sad days, great days, bad days? Could you write notes and pin them to your fridge to help remind you that things will get better? Do you have someone you can call, see or chat to on-line who can help remind you?

Try to think of ways to recognise, acknowledge and act upon symptoms that are negative or positive that can help you feel better in the long term.

Y is for…

Yoga, walking, exercise…

Doing some form of exercise has been proven to improve mental health. Of course you will only participate in a sport if you are fit and able to, and your doctor can help advise you on what would be suitable for you. I would highly recommend getting professional advice so that you do not cause yourself harm.

From walking, water aerobics and yoga, to racquet sports, cross training and running, there are many ways to exercise alone, with a partner or in a group; whatever takes your fancy!

Z is for…

Zzzz

Finally, and appropriately I feel, it's about getting enough sleep. Getting to bed a little earlier than usual, not using the computer or technology just before trying to go to sleep, exercising earlier in the day or evening, can all help. Drinking Camomile tea, having a warm bath, changing the bed clothes, can also lead to calm.

Everyone needs a different amount of sleep, so get to know your own needs and ensure that you try to get the rest you need. Depression and anxiety can get in the way of sleeping. I have spent countless nights in the past just lying there thinking and worrying. I began keeping a note pad and pen by my bedside, so that if anything important came into my head, I could write it down and forget about it until the morning.

And of course, lack of sleep can worsen depression and anxiety, so it can become cyclic yet again, so try to find the best way to help yourself get enough rest.

So, I have come to the end of my A – Z of coping skills for depression and anxiety and I would like to acknowledge the many other disorders/illnesses (mental and physical) that can co-occur with depression and anxiety including:

- Eating Disorders
- Self-Harm
- OCD
- Alcohol/substance issues
- IBS
- Under-active thyroid
- Headaches/Migraines

I have had to deal with all of these at various times in my life and I will talk about these in future books. For now, I shall leave you with a few more tips…

Positive thinking

I have been exercising positivity in a few different ways lately, to help me with my continuing journey of recovery, so I'd like to share a few more ways to do this. These may sound simple exercises but they work for me. These examples are not all from my own thoughts and feelings, but are more general.

First of all, it's the simply exercise of changing negative thoughts into positive thoughts…

I can't do it = I can do it

I'm a failure = I'm a success

Yes, yes, yes very simple but bear with me…

Now, onto turning negative thoughts into some positive action…

I can't get that job = apply and see what happens

I can't be a beautician = get signed up for a course

I'll never get a boyfriend = Well, are you in a position to find one at the present time? Do you actually want one? Then go from there…

Write two lists:

All the positive things about yourself (honest, thoughtful, like buying people presents, good at your job etc)

All the positive things in your life right now (friends, family, events, home, security)

Now write all the negatives…

There are a lot more positives than negatives right?

Another list that is good to make is about what is important to you; your ethics. For me, these are things like 'justice' and 'protecting the vulnerable, such as elderly, animals and children'

Making photo collages…

I bought two big plastic fronted clip frames years ago and had never used them. I had also been trying to put all my pictures up on the walls, but ran out of suitable frames, so I thought, let's make a collage – I haven't done that since I was a child. Now, I am always changing and moving stuff around in my home, and I am a (nearly) qualified in interior design (yep another thing I began and dropped out of near the end!). I love to design little spaces in my house, as I don't have much room.

So, I (being mindful) took all my left over pictures/paintings I have collected from abroad, childhood photos, recent photos, photos Chris bought from my 40th Birthday cruise last year, aerial and other photos I have taken of places and scenes, and put them all together in a frame. It came out so well, I made another one!

If you haven't much money to spare, then these are a great way to jazz up a wall and inspire good memories, and you can change them any time too and how about making one for someone special as a gift.

So now, when eating my dinner, I have some lovely photos and memories to ponder over and if anyone comes round, they make a good talking point.

Finally, my message is that **"YOU CAN DO IT TOO!"** Even if you do not suffer with mental illness, you are bound to know someone who does, if not more. I just want to spread the word that, although not all mental illnesses can be completely overcome, there is so much hope to manage symptoms and eradicate some to have 'a life worth living'. Hard work can pay off and it really is worth the fight – giving up should not be an option. And putting our recovery into someone else's hands should not be either. We have to help ourselves too – fight for our lives. Often we cannot get all the help we need from outside sources, so this is crucial sometimes and we should take responsibility for ourselves, it's very rewarding.

Keeping up with me!

You can find all my latest news through my blog/website or various social networks:

Blog/website: http://www.amandagreenauthor.co.uk

Facebook: https://www.facebook.com/AmandaGreenAuthor

Twitter: https://twitter.com/AmandaGreenUK

Goodreads:
https://www.goodreads.com/AmandaGreenAuthorUK

I am also on LinkedIn, AuthorsDB and many other sites.

Other books by Amanda Green

Memoirs

'My Alien Self: My Journey Back to Me' (Memoirs of Amanda Green)

And

'39' (Memoirs of Amanda Green)

Short story books

'What I Know and two more short stories' (Amanda Green's Short Stories)

And

'The Woman Who Lives Next Door – A Short Story' (Amanda Green's Short Stories)

Novelette

'Living The Dream – A Novelette' (An Amanda Green Novelette)

Novella

'Behind Those Eyes: Life on the Streets of London' (An Amanda Green Novella)

Printed in Great Britain
by Amazon